T0307168

Praise for *To Invest Successfully*

"When I started investing, I didn't know a put from a putt. Finding all today's financial terms so well defined and organized was truly beneficial."

—R. J. McKinley, Board Director, Global Ad Agency

"The author, Edith Lynn Hornik-Beer, begins with an example of a young couple talking to their financial advisor about their investments. She uses this example to illustrate the need for most of us who are not familiar with investing to easily access information on the myriad financial products available, including less-known terms. It is very helpful to have a book that provides simple definitions and explanations of financial terms that can arm us with the necessary knowledge we need to make sound financial decisions. This book has and will stand the test of time as a seminal book of advice on this topic."

—R. Gannon-Cook, coauthor of *Engaging learners with semiotics: Lessons learned from reading the signs*

"Edith Hornik-Beer brings not only a seasoned author's skills to the task of providing this invaluable compendium of investment terms, she also brings her in depth and well-earned investment knowledge and experience to the task. This book is an essential tool for anyone wading into the investment world."

—Sandra Lamb, author of *How to Write It* and *Writing Well for Business Success*

"With an insightful, concise, and convenient style, Edith Lynn Hornik-Beer's book approaches readers from non-financial backgrounds to business professors and seasoned CEOs. This book is a must-read, friendly guide for potential investors authored by a careful researcher and exceptional communicator. Edith uses her unique and impactful writing style to immerse the reader into an illustrative and thought-provoking use of financial terms."

—Dr. Rafael Perez, Associate Professor of Business at Colorado Mountain College

"*To Invest Successfully: Terms You Need at Your Fingertips* is the perfect companion for an investor who wants concise up-to-date information on investment terms."

—Priscilla Jones, immigration attorney

To Invest
Successfully

To Invest Successfully

Terms You Need at Your Fingertips

Edith Lynn Hornik-Beer

OPEN ROAD
INTEGRATED MEDIA
NEW YORK

Published in 2024 by Open Road Integrated Media, Inc.
180 Maiden Lane
New York, NY 10038
www.openroadmedia.com

CONTENTS

INTRODUCTION

I was waiting in my bank to see one of the vice presidents when I overheard the following conversation between one of the bank's advisors and a young couple who were obviously considering investments.

Banker: "Let's see how much money you have to invest and if we should set you up with one of our financial advisors."

The young woman: "Excuse me but what would the advisor present to us?"

Banker: "Different investment choices. For example, there are annuities if you are thinking about your retirement age."

The young man: "I am thinking of a nest egg for a rainy-day situation."

The young woman: "Could you explain annuities? Since we have received this small inheritance I was hoping for some monthly income."

Banker: "Annuities are one option. But if you want temporary income you might consider commercial papers."

The young woman: "I hate to interrupt again, but is there a list of all the different types of investments?"

Banker: "There are lists. I am sure you have heard of stocks, bonds, cryptocurrency, precious metals such as gold. You may want to study each category."

And there I thought is a real need, a list of financial terms that investors could have at their fingertips before they invest in bonds, stocks, the money instrument market, cryptocurrency, real estate or anything else in the world of finance.

At this point you might ask what about the internet? You know, Google for a quick why and wherefore. The answer is where business investment is concerned it is never one word but a series of words, a classed grouping. Here is a concrete example. You probably know the word bond. But you want a solid definition. You look it up online under business. A definition of what the word bond means in the business world pops up. There will probably also pop up a list of the popular bonds and institutions which sell them. But you don't get the other vocabulary you need at your fingertips to explain what you hope to get out of a bond investment. Such words as par, long coupon, premium bond, extension swap, or effective yield are only a small sample of words that help you to invest successfully in bonds.

Assume this young couple had had a list and a simple definition of every type of business investment and all the terms related to each type of investment at their fingertips. They could express better their particular needs when talking to the banker. They also would know what alternatives are available if their financial advisor does not offer them what they want.

To Invest Successfully: Terms You Need at Your Fingertips covers each financial subject such as stocks, money instruments, cryptocurrency, real estate, insurance and loans in separate chapters. The words in each chapter are in alphabetical order so that you can not only find a term within a subject quickly but also get a feel of all the terms needed to express yourself well on that particular subject. This book is only intended to expose and define financial language and not to advise the reader how to invest. The most important words are included, all defined in clear-cut words.

Suppose you come across a word that piques your interest and you don't know to which category it belongs. You simply look the word up in the index which will guide you to the proper chapter.

Our recent and continual economic fluctuations have given birth to many new financial terms. Other terms are not as new, but seem to be because we are using them more due to present financial and economic situations.

Whether new, rarely used or often used, these terms have all been gathered in this book and defined in clear and simple terms. Hopefully it will make the ins and outs of the financial world and its jargon more meaningful.

One more IMPORTANT notice: The author has included links to important associations, organizations and government agencies which deal with specific financial aspects important to the investors. Just the way phone numbers or addresses may be changed, we have to realize hyperlinks occasionally may have their contact link changed. Should you receive a 404 error, if the group still exists, Google will most likely be able to provide the new link.

To Invest
Successfully

BONDS

AAA or Aaa: the highest-quality rating a bond can receive. The ratings are given by several independent rating services, two of which are Moody's Service and S&P Global Inc., previously known as Standard & Poor's.

accretion: a bond's rise in principal value to full face value at maturity. This rise occurs when a bond is purchased below face value. *See* face value, deep discounted bond and discount bond

accrued interest: interest earned but not yet due and payable. For example, if a bond paying interest on January 1 and July 1 is bought on February 3, the buyer will receive on July 1 an interest payment for one half year. Since the seller owned the bond for thirty-four days of that six-month period, the seller will still receive the interest accrued during those thirty-four days.

amortization: the principal money borrowed in a loan is paid down along with the interest due until the loan is paid off.

basis point: 1/100 of 1 percent yield. Fifty basis points would mean 0.5 percent.

basis price: price expressed in terms of yield to maturity, also known as annual rate of return. A case in point is a five-year bond whose yield is 10 percent. During the bond's lifetime the country's prime rate goes down to 9 percent. Obviously, the bond's 10 percent yield would become valuable and increase the bond's price. The bond's yield as compared to other bonds' yields would be expressed in basis points. *See* prime rate

bond: an interest-bearing certificate of debt usually issued by a government or corporation which obligates the issuer to pay the principal amount back at a specified time.

bond anticipation notes (BANS): notes issued by states and municipalities to procure interim financing for projects that will be eventually funded by long-term issues.

bond calendar: a schedule of newly issued bonds which will be available to the public shortly.

bond options: the right to buy (call) or sell (put) within a designated time on specified treasury bills, notes and bonds. The cost of money (interest rates) during the remaining life of the bond will determine the price.

callable bond: the issuer has the right to redeem the bond before the maturity date by paying some specified call price which is cited on the face of the bond certificate.

convertible bond: a bond which at the option of the holder may be converted into other securities of the corporation. Bonds are only convertible into those stocks which have been authorized at the time the bonds are issued.

corporate bond equivalent also known as equivalent bond yield: the annual yield on non-interest-bearing bonds (also bills, notes and short-term papers) adjusted to be comparable to the yield quoted on coupon-bearing obligations. The principle of equivalent yield also exists in our personal lives. If a friend came up to you and said, "Lend me $1,000 at 10 percent for one year and on the 365th day of the year I will pay you back not $1,000 but $1,100," you might answer, "I have that $1,000 in a 10 percent savings account which pays interest semiannually, and it is automatically reinvested so that I get compounded interest. Roughly speaking, in six months I'll get $50 interest, and by the end of the year the $50 will have earned me another $2.50. Therefore, $1,000 invested at 10 percent compounded earns me $102.50 and not $100 interest." Your friend might then reply, "Whatever you lend me I will give you an 'equivalent yield' except that I will pay you the sum at the end of the year."

coupon: a term for interest payment.

credit risk: the chances of loss because the issuer of a bond is not able to pay back completely or in part the principal and/or interest. *See* AAA

current coupon: coupons of those bonds issued in the past whose yield is more or less the same as the yield being offered on newly issued bonds. For example, Debbie Smith bought a bond two years ago which gave her a 10 percent yield. New bonds are yielding approximately 1/8 of 1 percent more. Debbie considers the bond she owns to be within the line of the current coupon offerings.

current issues: most recently offered bonds and notes.

current yield: the annual return of an investment.

cushion bond: sold at a premium price because of a relative higher return which protects the buyer against unexpected surge in market rates. However, the issuer has the option to pay off the debt early.

debenture bond: an unsecured bond backed only by the credit standing of the issuer rather than by specific property or mortgage. Government bonds are usually unsecured since generally their only backing is taxes. *See* revenue bond and special assessment bond

deep discount bond: a bond which is considerably below maturity price, giving the investor an opportunity for a long-term gain. For example, several years ago John Colt bought a $1,000 bond paying 6 percent interest and due in ten years. John Colt had no way of knowing when he locked his money into a 6 percent yield that interest rates would go sky-high. His accountant is now suggesting that he sell his bond because he could use the loss on his income tax. John Colt's $1,000 bond is now selling on the bond market for $842. The new buyer will continue to receive $60 annually or 6 percent of $1,000. But because the new buyer bought the bond for only $842 he is actually receiving 10 percent on his investment. Even though he only paid $842 for the bond, he will receive the full $1,000 at maturity.

default: failure to fulfill a contract such as interest or principal due at the designated time.

discount bond: a bond sold at a price lower than its face value.

dollar bond: a bond issued outside of the United States priced in dollars and paying in dollars. May also refer to USA government bonds.

effective yield: the yield of the principal (gain or loss) plus the interest of a bond bought at above or below par calculated at maturity when there is a capital gain or loss as well as interest income. *See* par

eurobond: when spelled with a capital E, Eurobond is a bond issued by Eurozone countries. When spelled with a small e, it represents a bond issued in a currency foreign to the country where it was issued. For example, a bond issued in Japanese yens in the United States would be a eurobond. These eurobonds are then denominated in euros.

extension swap: prolonging a bond's maturity through swapping for a similar one with a longer current maturity. The swap may also be accomplished by selling a bond just before its due date, when it may tend to be slightly above par, and buying a similar bond with a longer maturity date. *See* par

face value: the amount the company issuing the bond promises to pay at maturity.

Fannie Mae Debt Securities: a nickname for Federal National Mortgage Association, founded in 1938 as a government sponsored corporation which has a varied history. Fannie Mae Bonds are mortgage-backed securities and are considered a safe investment by many bond investors. Today due payments of principals are backed by federally insured or guaranteed loans. The loans are a beneficial ownership interest in either a single mortgage loan or a pool of mortgage loans secured by residential properties and are guaranteed as to timely payment of principals and interest by Fannie Mae. For more information visit:

www.fhfa.gov/about-fannie-mae-freddie-mac

capitalmarkets.fanniemae.com/mortgage-backed-securities

Federal Home Loan Mortgage Association also known as Freddie Mac: constituted by the federal government in 1970 to support the mortgages of middle-income Americans. For more information visit: www.bankrate.com/mortgages/fannie-mae-vs-freddie-mac/#what-are. Freddie Mac are mortgage-backed securities and are considered a safe investment by many bond investors.

www.fhfa.gov/about-fannie-mae-freddie-mac

fixed-dollar security: non-negotiable instrument such as bank deposits and government savings bonds that can be redeemed at a fixed price at some predetermined fixed schedule.

flat trades also known as flat income bond: a bond in default and therefore without accrued interest. Some corporate revenue which are not in default and also trade without interest.

floating-rate bond: a bond whose yield is adjusted every six months to bring the bond into line with the current market rate.

funded debt: debts secured by committing specific assets to a sinking fund. *See* sinking fund

general obligation bond: municipal security whose credit rating is determined by its taxing powers, past credit rating and reputation.

gilt-edged bond: a highly-rated bond (*see* AAA) whose issuer has a long reputation for paying interest without interruption.

Ginnie Mae: a nickname for Government National Mortgage Association. An agency for all government guaranteed or insured mortgages within the Department of Housing and Urban Development.
www.ginniemae.gov

give up swap: the loss that occurs when a block of bonds is swapped for another block offering lower coupon yields. This may be done to incur a loss needed for taxes.

governments: another term for negotiable US Treasury securities.

guaranteed bond: a bond whose interest and/or principal is guaranteed by a company other than the issuer. The guarantee does not necessarily appear on the face of the bond but may be in a separate agreement.

income bond: a bond which repays the principal but only pays interest when earned. Sometimes the accumulated unpaid interest may be claimed against the corporation when the bond becomes due.

indenture of a bond: the written agreement under which bonds are issued. An indenture contains the maturity date, interest rate and other terms. The term comes from an obsolete custom of placing the copies of an agreement together and tearing an irregular edge on one side. Matching of the edges of any two documents at a later date was considered proof of the identity of the documents containing the agreements.

junk bond: a bond in default, or a bond considered high-risk because of low rating.

long bond: a bond whose maturity is many years off.

long coupon: a bond which may have more than one interest due date, but which has one date in particular (usually the first coupon) which has a longer period to its due date than others or than is standard. *See* short coupon

market value: the present trade value of a bond.

marketability: the readiness with which one can trade a bond.

maturity: the date a bond, note or other indebtedness becomes due and payable.

minimum legal capital: the amount a corporation is required to keep in the business for the protection of the creditors. Usually it is the par value of the total issued certificate of debts. Each state has its own regulations.

modified pass-through mortgage securities: are bonds issued mostly by the government where the amount paid to the investor on a specified date is a combination of interest earned on the invested amount and whatever principal was paid off (pass-through) on the underlying mortgages.

mortgage bond: property, equipment or other real assets pledged as security. If a corporation is forced to default in the payment of its bonds, secured obligations possess priority to the extent of the value of the property pledged. Not to be confused with a general mortgage bond, which may be outranked by one or more other mortgages.

municipal notes (MUNI): short-term notes issued by munici-palities in anticipation of funds from bond issues, receipts or other proceeds.

odd lot: a term used in the bond market when less than one trading unit or less than even units are purchased. *See* round lot

OID: (original issue discount): newly issued bond sold as if it were a discount bond. *See* discount bond

par: the face value of a security at maturity or the amount at which a debt security contracts to pay out at maturity. Often signifies the dollar value upon which interest will be paid.

par bond: a bond selling at face value.

pass-through rate also known as net interest rate: the interest paid to investors after management fees, servicing costs are deducted by the issuer.

paydown: as payments are made each time to pay off a debt the paydown is the percentage of principal paid off to the lender compared to the total principal owed.

pay-up: 1) any borrower's willingness to pay a higher rate in order to get funds; 2) the loss of cash incurred by swapping into higher-priced bonds.

pick-up: the term for a higher yield when bonds are swapped for another block of bonds offering higher coupons.

point: a term used to quote the change in the price of a bond. One point represents $10 or a percentage of $1,000, so that a bond which rises three points gains 3 percent of $1,000 or $30 in value. An advance from ninety-five to ninety-eight would mean in dollars from $950 to $980 for each $1,000 bond.

premium: 1) the difference between the face value and the actual higher price at which an issue is trading; 2) the amount paid in excess of the face value in order to call a bond before maturity.

premium bond: a bond selling above par.

prepayment: a payment made ahead of the scheduled payment date.

presold issue: a bond issue which is sold out before it reaches the market.

principal: the face amount of a bond; commonly known as par value.

puttable bond: permits redemption before due date usually on one or more indicated dates.

RANs: abbr. Revenue Anticipation Notes. Issued by states and cities to finance current expenses in anticipation of income from nontax sources. For example, a municipal stadium may be financed by RANs with the thought that the stadium's income will pay off the notes.

rating: worthiness of a bond. *See* AAA

red herring: a preliminary prospectus filed with the SEC (*see* SEC) before securities may be issued. The prospectus is marked with red ink: "Not a solicitation, for information only."

refunding: a new issue of bonds to replace existing bonds. *See* paydown

registered bonds: a bond whose owner is registered with the issuer; the name of the owner also appears on the face of the bond, and the proceeds are payable only to the owner.

regular way settlement: the schedule as determined by regulators of the market in question as to when the buyer has to complete payment or when the seller needs to deliver the assets traded.

reinvestment rate: 1) the rate at which an investor can reinvest interest payments received from coupons or other securities; 2) the rate at which proceeds from a sale or maturity of a bond can be reinvested in the present market.

relative value: comparison of one bond to another in terms of relative maturity, interest, yield, risk, liquidity and return.

revenue bond: a municipal bond backed by revenues from rents, charges or tolls.

round lot also known as full lot: a term for trading units. In bonds a round lot is usually $100,000 worth.

seasoned issue: a term used for bonds issued by established reputable companies; has a good resale value and sold well when originally issued.

SEC: abbr. Securities and Exchange Commission. An arm of the federal government created to protect the investor against malpractice and misinformation in the securities market. All new bond and stock issues must be registered with the SEC, which enforces disclosure rules on all new security issues and supervises the activities of all investment companies and counselors in the United States.
www.sec.gov
See Office of Investor Education and Advocacy

secondary market: the market where bonds and other securities are resold.

sector: bonds similar in type, maturity, rating and/or coupons.

serial bonds: bonds issued at the same time but that mature serially (staggered dates) and usually with interest rates varying for the different maturity dates.

series bonds: groups of bonds usually issued at different times and with different maturities (Series A, Series B). These bonds are under the authority of the same indenture.

shopping: when selling or seeking a bond, attempting to obtain the best price by calling several dealers.

short bond: a bond having a short current maturity.

short coupon: coupons or interest due to the bond owner very shortly; a coupon payment period below the usual 180 days.
See long coupon

sinking fund: the sum set aside out of the company's earnings to pay off an issue of bonds. The company will either purchase or call the bonds according to the terms of the indenture. Part of the written agreement under which bonds are issued may require a sinking fund.

special assessment bond: a bond backed by the power of the government to assess particular individuals for benefits presumably received in the form of public improvements financed by the bond issue.

take out: 1) to sell a block of bonds or securities and buy another block at a lower price, thus generating funds. For example, if John Smith decided to sell his bond at $1,100 and buy a new one at $1,000 par, his takeout would be $100; 2) to take the owner of the securities completely out of the market. This term is used by bond brokers or security brokers.

tax & revenue anticipation notes (TRANs): similar to TANs, except the source of revenue may be taxes and other revenues such as federal aid. *See* TANs

tax anticipation notes (TANs): notes issued by the government to provide funds for expenditures until taxes or other revenues can pay off the notes.

term bond: the time between a bond's issuance and its maturity at which point the principal amount is repaid to the bond holder.

times interest earned also known as interest coverage ratio: the calculation of how well a firm can pay its interest on an outstanding debt by dividing the earnings (before its interest and taxes are paid out) by its interest expenses for a given time.

treasury bill or note also known as T-bill: a non-interest bearing discount security issued by the US Treasury to finance the national debt. The income in discount bills is in the increase between the purchase price, which is discounted, and the full maturity value. If, for instance, the Treasury decides to offer issues of $1,000 notes discounted at 10 percent, the purchaser would only pay $900 (10 percent of $1,000 equals $100; $1,000 less $100 equals $900) and receive $1,000 at maturity.

trust: certificates denoting that one owns the bond or the coupon of a particular US Treasury bond which is held by a trustee.

www.treasurydirect.gov/savings-bonds/cashing-a-bond/trusts

US Dollar Bonds: a bond issued outside the United States by a corporation or government in US dollars and not in the foreign country's currency.

US Savings Bonds: a term that usually refers to a series of bonds issued by the federal government. Depending on the series these bonds are available in various sums starting at $50 or less.

www.treasurydirect.gov/savings-bonds/buy-a-bond

visible supply: the amount of municipal bond issues scheduled within the next thirty days will indicate how much new debt is expected to come to market. An overflow may cause a bear market. *See* bond calendar; *see* bear market

when issued trades (WI): a term referring to the period when a bond is announced and sold but has not yet been issued; the bond is traded "when, as, and if issued."

yankee bond: a foreign bond issued in the United States, registered with the SEC (*see* SEC) and payable in dollars.

yield curve: a graph showing, as of a predetermined date, the different yields to maturity on bonds similar in every respect except their maturity.

yield to maturity: the calculation of a bond's annual return from the principal, plus annual interest, at a fixed future date. Bond yield tables are available.

zeros: a discounted bond issued without a coupon.

STOCK MARKET TRADING TERMS

arbitrage: the purchase of foreign exchange, stocks, bonds, silver, gold, or other commodities in one market for sale in another market. For example, one can purchase gold on the London market and sell it on the Paris market; similarly, exchanges of securities may also take place in a merger.

auction market: another term for the various stock exchange markets where buyers and sellers compete with each other for the most advantageous price.

authoritarian: a term describing an investing approach whereby the investor makes the selection of stocks by following the lead of assumed experts.

averages: a term used for the various rather elaborate formulas to measure stock trends. The formulas include stock splits and stock dividends, which are not to be confused with dollar cost averaging. *See* Dow Jones Industrial Average

balance sheet: a company's annual financial statement including the assets, debts, liabilities, available capital and stockholders' interest in the company.

bear: one who thinks the market will decline.

bear market: a term signifying a decline in the market.

bid and asked: the bid is the price offered at any time for a security or commodity, and the ask is the price requested. The quote, also known as the quotation, is the bid and asking on a security or commodity. For instance, a quote on a given stock may be 20.25 bid and 20.50 asked. In other words, the highest price a buyer wanted to pay was $20.25, and the lowest the seller was willing to take was $20.50.

Big Board: a term for the New York Stock Exchange.

block: a large amount of stock in round numbers, popularly considered to be 10,000 or more.

blue chip: a stock that is low-risk because the company has a reputation for reliability, quality and the ability to make money and pay dividends.

blue sky laws: laws enacted by various states to protect the public against security frauds. The expression supposedly originated with a judge who ruled that a particular stock held as much value as a patch of blue sky.

board room: the room in a club or broker's office where leading stock prices are displayed electronically or on a ticker tape. Before the days of electricity and the internet the prices were posted on a board.

book also known as trading book: basically refers to an accounting kept by all types of financial institutions and stockbrokers, detailing their clients' transactions for whom they have acted as the broker or middleman for dealing in securities. *See* designated market maker

book value: an accounting term used to denote a company's assets.

broker: an agent who has passed a test to determine his basic knowledge in securities, who is registered with the SEC (*see* SEC) and who may charge a fee to buy and sell securities, commodities, and other properties for the public.

bull: one who believes the market will rise.

bull market: the term used to express a rise in the market.

buy-and-hold strategy: holding onto stocks and other securities during all market fluctuations.

call: the right to buy a fixed amount of stock at a specified price within a given time.

callable preferred stock: preferred stock that may be redeemed by the issuing corporation.

capital stock: all stocks in a business including common and preferred; also refers to the amount of stocks a corporation may issue and that amount is recorded on its balance sheet.

cash sale: a cash transaction on the floor of the stock exchange which calls for delivery of the securities the same day. Deliveries usually take five days.

certificates: the papers denoting ownership of a security. The certificates use watermarked paper and delicate etchings to make forgery difficult. Unless the certificate is registered with a company or broker, loss of a certificate may be irredeemable.

churning: a method to generate brokerage commissions; an unethical and in some cases illegal practice of trading and turning over a customer's securities faster than necessary, purportedly for the customer's good.

closed end funds: a fixed number of shares usually devoted to a single sector or industry sold through a single initial public offering (IPO); www.investopedia.com/terms/i/ipo.asp. This fixed number may be resold in various quantities on a stock market.

commission: the fee charged to the public for purchasing or selling securities or commodities. The agent who carries out the public orders is known as a commission broker.

common stock: securities which represent an ownership interest in a company allowing certain voting rights. Management considers the stockholder when dividend payments, stock dividends, stock splits, recapitalizations, mergers, expansion, sale of new securities and use of rights are normally planned. Common stockholders assume a greater risk because their claims are junior to bondholders and other creditors of the company. The preferred stockholder is limited to a fixed dividend and in case of liquidation of assets has prior claim on dividends. However, the common stockholder may reap greater profits in the form of capital appreciation, dividends and extra declared dividends.

competitive trader also known as registered trader: a member of the exchange who trades in stocks on the floor for an account in which he has an interest. A trader is required to have passed the Securities Trader Representative Examination.

conglomerate: the result of mergers and takeovers of companies and corporations in complex deals involving cash and/ or securities, and culminating in the production of diversified, non-related items and services. The parent company may cite savings in common facilities, personnel and general staff services. The diversification promises a larger economic base for the stockholders, participation in new growth areas and in some instances an avoidance of the cyclical effect of a single industry. *See* merger

consolidated balance sheet: *see* Financial Statement Chapter

convertible preferred stock: stock that may be exchanged by the owner for common stock or another security, usually of the same company, as determined by the original issue.

covering: paying for a security previously sold short. *See* short selling.

cumulative preferred: preferred stocks which provide that if one or more dividends are omitted, these omitted dividends must be paid before dividends are paid on common stocks.

cumulative voting: the right of a shareholder to cast as many votes as the amount of shares the shareholder owns. The shareholder may cast these votes for each director, or the accumulated amount for one director, or divide among any number of them. For instance, Mary Smith owns 1,000 shares in XYZ Company. She is sent a list of ten nominees to the board of directors. She may cast 100 votes for each director or 1,000 votes cumulatively. She may decide to give her vote of 1,000 to one director or divide her voting rights into 300, 300, 300 and 100 thus voting for only four persons.

day order: an order to buy or sell that lasts only for the day it was placed. If it is not executed by the end of the day, the order is canceled.

dealer: an agent who buys over-the-counter stocks for his own account and sells to a customer from his inventory. Any security may be bought or sold by any securities firm which cares to do so. The bulk of such business is done in securities that are not actively traded on the stock exchanges. Dealers belong to the Financial Industry Regulatory Authority, an association of brokers and dealers in the over-the-counter securities business. FINRA has the power to expel members who have been found to be unethical.

debit balance: in a margin account, the portion of stocks unpaid and owed to the broker. *See* margin account

depository trust and clearing corporation (DTC): the central securities certificate depository where security deliveries are done by computerized bookkeeping, often avoiding the physical movement of stock certificates for the financial markets.

designated market maker (previously known as specialist): a member of the New York Stock Exchange or other exchanges who manages and keeps track of sector focused orders of stocks. A DMM may be responsible for trading in several specific dedicated stocks. If necessary, he/she/the firm buys and sells on their own account to maintain a balance of supply. A DMM must make a market in the stock they trade by displaying their best bid and ask prices to the market during trading hours. ETFs have mostly replaced DMMs. *See* ETF and bid

directors: those who supervise the managers of a corporation, bank or other business institution. Federal and state laws prescribe as to who may and may not be elected director to certain types of business institutions. For example, New York State Business Corporation Law (SEC 701) states that each member of the board of directors shall be at least twenty-one years of age. Federal and state laws in general define a director's rights, duties, restrictions and responsibilities. Directors are elected by shareholders and decide, among other matters, if and when dividends shall be paid. *See* SEC

discretionary account: an account set up by the customer that allows the broker in part or fully to decide the purchases or sales of securities or commodities, including selection, timing, amount, and price to be paid or received.

diversification: spreading one's investments among different companies in different fields.

dividends: the amount of payment decided by the board of directors to be made to the shareholder for each share held. Preferred shareholders generally receive a fixed amount which was determined when the preferred share was issued. *See* preferred stocks

dividend return: *see* financial statements

dollar cost averaging: taking a fixed dollar amount at regular intervals and buying stocks whether they are up or down; a means of building up equity in the stock market.

Dow Jones Industrial Average: a stock market average reached by a rather complicated formula. The average is calculated on the basis of thirty major publicly traded industrial companies on the NY Stock Exchange and NASDAQ.

earnings per share: figured by dividing a company's net profits by their outstanding shares of its common stock. The accounting may make adjustments for unusual items and situations.

equity: in stocks, the term is synonymous with the liquidation value of the company.

ETF: an assemblage of securities bought and sold on a stock exchange as if an individual stock. For example, the assemblage might be a collection of energy stocks or a stock containing a variety of categories picked because they all pay dividends or picked because they are all start-ups.

exchange acquisition: a way to buy a large block of stock on the floor of the exchange; the broker can solicit the various sell orders and ask to have them lumped together and matched with a large buy order. The price to the buyer may be net or on a commission.

exchange distribution: a way for a broker to sell a large block of stock by lumping together many small orders for the same stock. The commission is built into the price.

ex-dividend: means without dividend, because of the scheduling of the dividend; dividends are declared quarterly; as of a given date, sellers keep the most recent dividend and buyers get the next declared dividend.

ex-rights: means without rights. A corporation may issue more stock to raise money, and offer the right to its stockowners to buy additional stock at a discount from the prevailing market price. There are only a given number of rights per share that the stockholder may sell, thus owning the stock without rights.

extra: extra dividend issued in the form of stock or cash.

FINRA: abbr. Financial Industry Regulatory Authority. A non-profit organization that is not part of the United States government that licenses and regulates dealers and brokers of securities and financial instruments. www.finra.org

floor: the trading area on the New York Stock Exchange.

floor broker: a member of the stock exchange who can buy or sell any listed security on the floor and who may execute orders for his or her firm. Today's orders may be executed electronically.

formula investing: investing according to one of many theories on economic waves, cycles and other techniques. *See* fundamentalist, authoritarian, diversification, and technical analysis

fundamentalist: an approach to investing in which the selection of stocks is based on value, quality and yield or growth.

good delivery: delivery of an unencumbered security complying with the contract of sale and transfer title to the purchaser.

good 'til canceled order also known as GTC or open door: an order placed by a broker to buy or sell at a specific price that remains open until executed or withdrawn.

growth stock: a stock of a company whose earnings are at a faster growth rate than the Gross National Product. *See* gross national product

hedging: an effort to stabilize the value of a stock by selling or buying for future fulfillment.

inactive stock: a stock having a low volume of trade.

in and out: a purchase and sale of a security within a short time of each other. The trader is usually interested in a quick profit.

independent broker: a broker who has a seat on the stock exchange and will execute orders for those firms who do not have a seat or for those brokers who have more business than they can handle.

institutional investor: any large accumulation of capital for investment such as pensions or trusts of large organizations including universities, banks, insurance companies, etc.

investment banker: the middleman between the corporation issuing new securities and the public. The investment banker buys outright the new issue which is then sold to individuals and institutions. Thereafter the issue is traded in one of the securities markets.

investment company: a firm that sells stocks to investors and uses that capital to invest in other companies to achieve capital growth and capital gain. Investment companies sell two types of stocks: closed-end, which are salable on the open market, and open-end, which can only be sold back to the issuing investment company. As a rule investment companies are registered with the SEC.

Investors Service Bureau: a service provided by the New York Stock Exchange answering all written inquiries concerning stock investments. The bureau's services include clarification of exchange operations, and advice on tracing allegedly fraudulent securities.

www.sec.gov/reportspubs/investor-publications/investor-pubs-aboutoiea

IPO: abbr. Initial Public Offering. Newly initiated securities sold to the public for the first time or what is called the primary market.

letter stock funds also known as restricted stock: unregistered stock purchased at 25–50 percent below market price; the shares are non-transferable until the company prospers so that the shares can be offered publicly at a profit in compliance with special Securities and Exchange Commission (SEC) regulations. As a rule these stocks are issued to executives and directors of the corporation.

leverage: ratio between common stock equity and debt. For example, equity of 10 percent and 90 percent debt would be highly leveraged.

limited price order: an order to either buy or sell securities only at a specified price.

liquidity: in the stock market, the ability of a security to withstand buying and selling at reasonable price changes.

load: the cost of commissions and distribution of mutual funds; the cost is incurred in purchases but usually not in sales.

long position: another way of expressing ownership of securities; "I am long 250 IBMs."

margin account: a type of account where a customer borrows money to pay for a certain percentage of the cost of securities. The margin is the money borrowed. The broker may use his or her credit to borrow the money from the bank for the customer's account; there is a charge for borrowing this money. The broker holds the securities for the customer as collateral. The Federal Reserve sets the maximum amount which may be borrowed. Margin requirements may be lowered to induce more trading or raised if the government fears overbuying or speculation fever. Margin accounts are risky because if the stock goes down, the customer is required to add money to maintain the margin.

margin call: request to the customer to put up collateral in the form of securities or cash with the broker. The call is made when the borrowed amount exceeds the amount the government allows a client to borrow.

market order: an order to buy or sell securities at the best price available to the customer at the time the order is placed.

market price: the most recent price at which a security has been sold.

Member Corporation: a securities brokerage firm, organized as a corporation, with at least one member of the New York Stock Exchange as a director and a holder of voting stocks in the corporation.

Member firm: When the brokerage firm is organized as a partnership with at least one general partner who is a member of the New York Stock Exchange, Inc., the firm is known as a Member Firm.

merger: the taking over by a stronger company of a more passive company by direct acquisition of the other's assets. The dominant company usually continues under the same name. No conglomeration is created by a merger. *See* conglomerate

Moody's Investor Service: a statistical service founded in 1909 by John Moody to determine ratings interrelated to stocks and bonds. Moody's services are used by private investors as well as banks, brokers, corporations, and every other conceivable financial institution.
ratings.moodys.io

mutual funds: a lineup of investment holdings managed by financial professionals which are available to shareholders.

NASDAQ: abbr. National Association of Securities Dealers Automated Quotations. The first electronic stock exchange. Based in New York City, it is especially known for trading in tech stocks.

net asset value per share: figure used by investment companies to compute their company's worth by totaling the market value of all securities owned. All liabilities are deducted and the balance divided by the number of shares outstanding. It is a calculation used for mutual funds, ETFs and closed end funds.

net change: the price change of a security from one day's closing hour to the next day's closing hour.

new issue: a new security being put on the market by a corporation.

New York Stock Exchange Common Stock Index: a means of calculating composite price movements of all common stocks listed on the Big Board.

no-load fund: an investment company that does not make a sales charge for the purchase of its shares.

nominee agreement: *see* Index

noncumulative: preferred stock whose unpaid dividends as a rule remain unpaid.

odd lot: stocks traded in units of under 100.

off board: a term used for securities not executed on a national securities exchange but rather over the counter.

Office of Investor Education and Advocacy: a help agency run by the USA government under the auspices of the SEC The agency provides user-oriented information about securities (including how to protect your investments) and will answer questions about suspected fraud, stock brokers' responsibilities and other unexpected related problems. *See* SEC www.investor.gov

open-end fund: a mutual fund investment company that continually issues shares as it receives new capital or that stands ready to redeem shares at net asset value.

option: the right to buy or sell at a specific price within a given time.

order good until a specified time: a limited price order which is to be canceled if not executed within a specified time. Jane Smith says she wants to buy 100 shares of XYZ stock provided the price goes down to $35 a share by the end of the week (Friday 4 P.M.); otherwise, the order is to be canceled. Ms. Smith has given an order good until a specified time.

overbought: a term describing a security which may rise in price because of sudden intense buying; some may be of the opinion that such a security may be overvalued or overbought. The reverse situation, when people sell a particular issue in quantity, causing a good security to go down in price, is known as oversold.

over-the-counter: method of issuing securities for those companies which may not meet the requirements for trading on the Big Board or their regional exchanges. The dealers may or may not be members of a securities exchange. OTC stocks usually are high risk stocks. *See* off board

par also known as the legal minimum value: the face value assigned to the share by the company's corporate charter; does not determine the market value of the common stock. Par may often signify the dollar value upon which dividends on preferred stocks are computed. Not to be confused with par bond.

participating preferred: preferred stock which receives dividends but is so chartered that once the common stockholders receive their dividends, the preferred stockholders receive extra dividends when possible.

passed dividend: omission of scheduled dividend.

payout ratio: dividends per share divided by the earnings per share or what percentage of their earnings a company pays out in dividends.

penny stocks: stocks selling at less than $3 a share. These are mostly over-the-counter stocks and may be speculative.

percentage order: an order to buy or sell a certain amount of a security only after a fixed number of shares have already been traded.

point: in stocks, one point represents $1. If a stock goes up 1.5 points it gains $1.50. If a stock goes down two points it loses $2. Not to be confused with bond points.

preferred stock: stock promising prior claim on the company's earnings. Dividends are paid at a specified time before common stock shareholders receive theirs, and in case of liquidation, preferred stockholders have priority in all claims.

premium: the surplus paid above the price the stock was originally issued.

price-earnings ratio: the formula between the company's stock price and earnings per share. There may be various reasons why a company's stock price may be low compared to its high earnings or why a stock price may be high even though its earnings are low.

primary distribution: the original sale of newly issued securities.

prospectus: the circular disclosing important material about new securities which must be given to the investor to protect the investor. New securities must be registered with the Security Exchange Commission. *See* SEC

proxy: written authorization given by the shareholder that someone else may represent him or her and vote the shares. A basis that enables an investor to vote without being in person at the meeting.

proxy statement: pertinent information required by the SEC (*see* SEC) for stockholders about the stock and their right to vote when solicited for their proxies.

quotation also known as quote: the highest bid to buy and the lowest offer to sell a security on the market. The quote tells you how your stock is doing.

record date: the date on which a stockholder must be registered on the stock book of a company in order to still receive dividends in that quarter and to be able to vote on any company affairs.

red herring: *see* Index.

registered representative also known as customer's man,

account executive or customer's broker: an employee working with securities who has met the requirements of the New York Stock Exchange regarding knowledge of the securities business.

registrar: the one in charge, such as a bank or trust company, that maintains the necessary records of the transactions of investors, including the current buy and sell, and ensures that not more are bought than available.

registration: procedure required by the Securities Act of 1933 that before new securities may be offered by a company, the securities must be registered.

regular way delivery: when payment is due on stock purchases, ETFs and mutual funds as regulated by the SEC. *See* SEC

right(s): privilege of shareholders to buy additional securities in the company ahead of the general public and at a reduced price whenever the company wants to raise money. The stockholder has a certain number of rights per share which he or she may sell rather than use.

round lot: a unit of trading. In the New York Stock Exchange a unit is generally 100 shares. In some inactive stock the unit is ten shares.

seller's option: right given by the New York Stock Exchange for the seller to deliver stocks or bonds any time within a specified period.

short position: a term for stocks sold short and not covered as of a certain date. Tom Smith believes stock XYC selling at $50 a share will go down to $30. He buys 100 shares at $30. On the due date XYC has gone down to $25 and Tom Smith has made $500. Had the stock gone down to only $35 Tom Smith would have lost $500.

short selling also known as short sales or short covering: rather than shares being bought first and sold later, the practice whereby shares are sold first and bought later in expectation that the market will go down. The broker "borrows" the stocks, sells them and holds the funds from the sale as collateral. The borrowed stock must be replaced by buying an equivalent amount (short covering) at a later date. If the stock goes down it will cost less to replace and a profit is made. There is an interest on the loan and stockbroker commission. One can do this transaction with stocks one already owns. For example, Mary Smith owns 200 shares of ABC which she feels will temporarily go down. She decides to borrow 100 of her own shares to sell short. This is known as selling short against the box.

sinking fund: *see* Index.

SIPC: abbr. Securities Investor Protection Corporation. A non-profit, non-government membership corporation which provides funds, when necessary, to protect member firms' customers' equity.

www.sipc.org

SPAC: abbr. Special Purpose Acquisition Company. Formed for the sole purpose of raising money through an initial public offering (IPO) to have the capital to merge or acquire another company. *See* IPO

special bid: an order to buy an unusually large block of stocks such as for a pension fund. The sale is regulated by expedient procedures such as making the sale on the floor of the exchange at a fixed price which may not be lower than the last or current sale of the security. The seller does not pay the commission.

special offering: a stock sale at a fixed price. The commission is included in the price. Allotments are made if there are more buyers than stock.

specialist: *see* Index

speculator: person willing to take risks, reasonable and not so reasonable, in the hope of making large gains.

split: agreement voted by the directors of the corporation and approved by its shareholders to divide the outstanding shares into a greater number of shares, such as 2 for 1; the equity remains the same. Carl Smith owns 100 shares of XZ stock selling for $50 a share. After the 2 for 1 split, Carl Smith owns 200 shares of XZ stock at $25 a share. If the stock goes up in value Carl Smith will have 200 shares instead of 100 shares which will go up in value.

Standard and Poor's (official name is S&P Global) Stock Price Indices: renowned for its many indices including its global ones. It is especially known for its S&P 500® of large cap US companies index which includes various sectors. This index is considered an indication of how well the American corporate economy is doing. For a list of indices visit: www.spglobal.com/spdji/en/index-finder

stock dividend: a dividend paid out in shares rather than cash. The shares may be of the issuing company or in a subsidiary of the issuing company.

stock exchanges: (not to be confused with stock market which is a collection of stock exchanges) a place where traders and stockbrokers buy and sell securities. The two largest in the world are NYSE New York stock Exchange and Nasdaq Stock Exchange, National Association of Securities Dealers Automated Quotations. For a complete list of world's exchanges visit en.wikipedia.org/wiki/List_of_stock_exchanges

stock option: the right to buy (call) or sell (put) stocks at a fixed amount, at a specified price within a given time.

　　1) A single call option gives the owner the right to buy 100 shares of a specific stock at a specific price (striking price) at any time prior to the expiration date. The price of the option (also known as premium) is the cost per

share with a minimum unit of 100. A quoted price of "one" means that one option on 100 shares of stock costs $100. Should the stock rise sufficiently to cover the cost of the premium before the expiration date, the owner will have made a profit. For example, XYZ stock costs $100 on the day Carl Smith takes an option for $10 to buy at that same price a month from now. XYZ rises to$200, but because Carl Smith contracted to buy at $100, he makes a profit of $100 less the premium he paid per share. In this case he has doubled his money. Had the stock gone down, he still would have had to pay the $100 and he would have lost the difference.

2) One can do the inverse: contract to sell (put) a specific stock. Suppose Carl Smith felt his XYZ bought at $100 had a good chance of going down in price. He can contract to sell (put) at $100 on the due date. If XYZ goes down to $80 a share, Carl makes a profit of $20 a share. Should the stock go up, he would lose money.

3) One can buy (call) and sell (put) another option of the same company; this is known as spread or straddle. Spreads or straddles can be a convenient way of spreading the risk or switching out of one option and into another. Assume Carl Smith had contracted to sell his XYZ stock and then realized that XYZ would have an excellent chance of actually going up in price. He could then straddle or spread his risk by putting in a separate call order due on another date.

Stock options can be bought and sold any time prior to the expiration date in much the same way as listed stock. The prices of the current stock options appear daily online. Because technology today can report the latest prices of options around the world from one minute to the next, newspapers and financial magazines no longer print a summary of the week's trades. It is best to get information from a trustworthy stockbroker specializing in stock options.

stock option contract: contract giving the purchaser the right to buy a number of shares of stock designated therein at a fixed price within a stated period of time.

stop limit order: stop is the price at which a person wants to buy or sell a stock or option; the trader (www.investopedia.com/terms/t/trader.asp) has control over when the order should be filled. However, if the stock/commodity does not reach the stop price during the specified time period the order can't be filled. The limit is the alternative. Mary Smith bought a stock at $75 a share. The stock has gone up to $95 a share. She says that if it reaches $110 she wants to sell (the stop) but if the stock goes down she still wants a profit and says it should be sold at $85 (the limit).

stopped stock: a guarantee to receive a stock at a certain current price with an opportunity to buy at a slightly more advantageous price. Such an order is executed by the broker and the specialist. Mary Smith wanted to have AB stock in her portfolio. The current price was 16½. Her broker asked the specialist to hold 100 shares at 16½, but should the stock go down to 16¼ (a savings of $25 for Mary), then the specialist would buy it at the lower price. Should the stock go up to 17 Mary has her stock guaranteed at 16½.

street name: the term for securities held in the broker's or brokerage firm's name and not in the customer's name. Sometimes customers prefer to have the stocks in the broker's name because, among many other reasons, they can be used as collateral when the customer wishes to buy on margin.

syndicate: a group of individuals and/or investment firms, banks and stockbrokers who are temporarily associated together under one manager for some specific business venture. For example, it may be to underwrite a particular security or to invest in a large real estate undertaking such as a shopping center or an office complex.

takeover: an acquisition of one corporation by another. It may be friendly or incur a proxy fight. In order to win, the acquiring company may offer a higher price than warranted for the available stocks. *See* merger

technical analysis: the practice of choosing the securities for one's portfolio not by how a corporation fares, but by the movement of the price of its stock as well as analyzing a myriad of patterns such as its history of dividends, earnings, assets, market trends and indexes.

10-K or 10-Q: a digital report form available to stockholders stating the annual (K) or quarterly (Q) financial results of those companies where they own stocks which are registered with the Securities and Exchange Commission.

tender offer: a request by a corporation under specific terms and for a certain time period for the public, and other stockholders such as institutions, to surrender their stocks usually at a price higher than the current market. There are different reasons that a company may grant a tender offer. One is to reward early investors and longtime employees by offering them liquidity.

The Uniform Prudent Investor Act: a law based on the original Prudent Man Rule and approved by the American Bar Association in 1995 stating that a fiduciary acting on behalf of another person or persons must put their clients' interest before his or her own. The law further specifies that the holdings should be protected by not speculating, by having diversified holdings and when need be the money management may be assigned to a third qualified party. There are more parts to the law and a minority of states have not accepted the law in its entirety.

thin market: a condition whereby there are few bids to buy or sell on the market as a whole or in one specific stock or area.

third market: *see* over-the-counter

time order: a limited price order at a specified time.

tip: supposedly inside information concerning the financial world.

top heavy: a term describing a market priced too high (for various reasons) and likely to decline.

trader: one who buys and sells for short-term profit.

treasury stock: stock issued by a corporation, reacquired by the corporation, and held in the company's treasury. Such stocks are not for sale to the public and have no voting rights and do not receive dividends.

turnover of working capital: within a given period, the amount of income in dollars produced by each dollar of net working capital.

underwriter: dealer or broker in an investment company who buys new issues from a corporation with the intent to resell these securities to the public.

unit investment trust: works similarly to a mutual fund but is only sometimes available. It is invested in all types of securities such as bank CDs, stocks and bonds. The fund is bought in units, matures at a set time, but may be sold anytime without a penalty; if interest rates go down, the unit goes up in value and sells at a profit. Unit investment trusts are set up to serve various purposes and some are tax exempt investments.

unlisted: description of a security not listed on one of the exchanges and therefore sold over the counter. Today admission of a stock to unlisted trading privileges requires SEC approval dependent on filed information. *See* SEC

warrant: a certificate giving the holder the right to purchase securities at a stipulated price within a specified period of time, or sometimes perpetually.

wire house: Originally a wire house was a member firm of an exchange maintaining a communication network linking (via telegram or telephone) either its own branch offices, the offices of correspondent firms or a combination of such offices. Today, because everyone has access to information through various communication systems such as the internet, the term has changed its meaning to denote a larger member firm with many branches.

working control: ownership of at least 51 percent of a company's stock—the minimum amount that one must own to exercise majority control in the company.

COMMODITIES

actual market: when a commodity such as sugar, oil, wheat, etc., is delivered without delay. *See* commodity cash market.

CDF: abbr. commercial deposit futures. Private debt instruments in which speculators buy futures. When money is tight rates rise. When money is available rates may decline.

CME: abbr. Chicago Mercantile Exchange Group. *See* New York Mercantile Exchange in this chapter

COMEX: The Commodity Exchange Inc. Primarily a future and option market for metals including gold and silver. COMEX has merged with NYMEX. *See* New York Mercantile Exchange in this chapter

commodities: there are two types of commodities: hard products, consisting of materials that are mined such as oil and gold, and soft products, such as soybeans, sugar, coffee, etc., which are traded at a price set in the future. If the commodity's future price is less than predicted, the purchaser loses money. Once the future contract has expired the trade is finished. The speculator either sells at the price or takes possession of the product.

www.usgs.gov/centers/national-minerals-information-center/ minerals-yearbook-metals-and-minerals

commodity cash market also known as spot or actual market: market for goods bought in large quantity for immediate delivery for actual use. For example, a chicken farm would buy chicken feed on a spot market. Cash prices are less than future prices because there are no insurance, storage or broker fees.

commodity exchanges: commodity exchanges are member organizations each with its own governing board which sees to it that business is carried out according to regulations. Non-members trade through brokerage firms which hold membership through partners or officers. There are globally over 100 exchanges. For a list of exchanges and what they trade go to:

www.jpx.co.jp/english

www.commoditiesx.co.uk/en

en.wikipedia.org/wiki/List_of_commodities_exchanges

commodity futures contract: a promise to buy or sell a certain amount of goods at an agreed price at a fixed future date.

commodity futures market: buying and selling for future delivery; some buy to speculate and sell before delivery.

commodity futures maturity date: delivery date.

Commodity Futures Trading Commission: protects the public from fraud, manipulation, and abusive practices related to the sale of commodity and financial futures and options. Fosters open, competitive, and financially sound futures and option markets.

www.cftc.gov/Contact/index.htm

commodity margin: the percentage of the conceptual amount the buyers must pay. The cash requirements for commodities trading are low: 5–10 percent, varying according to the commodity and to the broker's standards. There are no interest payments on the balance.

commodity options: calls (to buy) and puts(to sell) on commodity futures contracts. The speculator cannot lose more than the cost of the options. A commodity option is the right, not the obligation, to buy or sell a futures contract, at a fixed price for a certain period of time. Options may in a sense be a price insurance because the buyer only pays a one-time option premium (current market price). Of course if the price goes down the buyer loses money.

commodity short sale: a buyer sells a commodity when it is high and buys it back when it goes down in price. For example, Mary Ann borrows options of gold which are selling at $100 an ounce and sells their position. If the gold goes down to $50 an ounce Mary Ann buys it back and has made a profit of $50 an ounce. Of course if gold goes up to $150 Mary Ann loses money.

commodity speculators: those that play the commodity market to make money and who accept the risk hedgers want to avoid by taking positions in the market. *See* hedge

contract: agreement in a commodity trade that specifies the purchase price, quantity, date, and specified location; the minimum amount one can buy is one contract. The term comes from the early days when mainly agricultural products were traded and refers in part to the size it takes to fill a railroad car. Today one contract refers to a standardized amount that tells traders the exact quantities that are being bought or sold based on the terms of the contract.

daily price limits: how much or in what point range the market may move up or down within one trading day. Limits exist for the protection of speculators and member firms of the exchange.

delivery date: the date the commodity bought should be delivered; on the commodity market, the day the future contract expires.

genuine risk capital: money that an investor can afford to speculate without risking his livelihood, standard of living, or family.

hard products: *see* commodities

hedge: a means of preventing loss from price fluctuations; when a sale or a purchase is made involving a commodity, it is counterbalanced by a sale or purchase of the same commodity in the future.

light metals: *see* Index

long: to buy futures.

margin call: a request from the broker for more money if a future declines below the standard set.

New York Mercantile Exchange: The New York Mercantile Exchange (NYMEX) is the world's largest physical commodity futures exchange and encompasses today the Chicago Mercantile Exchange Group (CME Group).

scale order: the order given by the trader to sell or buy commodities at intervals; a buy or sell order at regular price is a spread of up or down to protect against loss. For example, 1,000 pounds of rice is bought at $1 a pound. If the futures go up ½ point, the order may be to sell half of the order then, and sell the other half when the future goes up another ½ point. This way the trader has made some profit at the first sale, so that if the price of rice should go down, the trader has some of the investment protected.

scalpers: those who buy and sell commodities for a small price difference with the intent of having gains from small price changes from large trade volumes.

short: to sell futures.

soft products: *see* commodities

spread: simultaneous purchase of a future for delivery in one month, and sale of a future in the same commodity for delivery in another month. There are different aspects to spread options. It may involve the differences between prices of the same commodity trading at two different locations (location spreads) or of different grades (quality spreads).

stop order: an order to buy or sell a commodity contract above or below a given price. If corn is selling at $6 a bushel, a stop order to sell can be put in to sell if it goes down to $5.50, thus minimizing the loss.

straddle: involving the same security to buy one contract and one to sell. There are many aspects to straddling, enough to fill a book. A farmer may sell half his crop at a price before harvest to guarantee his income. If at harvest the price for which he sold his crop is selling at a higher price he will lose income on the half he already sold, but had the guarantee of a certain amount of money. An investor may use these techniques differently hoping to make money on different soft and hard commodities.

www.investopedia.com/articles/optioninvestor/08/straddle-strategy.asp

straddle based on different stages of processing: purchase or sale of futures in equivalent quantities as, for example, December soybeans, soybean oil, soybean meal, etc.

strike: the price at which a put or call option can be carried out.

zero-sum game: another term for future market. The commodity market has for every up position a down position—thus making it a zero-sum game. For example, oranges may be up and wheat down. Not to be compared to the stock market, which has as a whole market up or down cycles.

MONEY INSTRUMENTS

Agency Discount Notes: short-term loans to federal government agencies which are bought through a broker. Instead of receiving interest, the notes are bought for less than they will pay at maturity. For example, a $1,000 six-month note may be bought for $900.

annualized average yield: an investment firm's average interest rate earned within a given period. The yield depends on operating expenses as well as the type of investments chosen by the directors.

annuity: a series of payments received in the future, most often from an insurance policy. Premiums, after having been paid for a series of years and which have during this time earned interest, are paid out in a lump sum or in installments during the rest of the beneficiary's life.

annuity certain also known as temporary annuity: income for a specified period of time, with the remaining payments going to a beneficiary if the annuitant dies.

Average Maturity Index of Money Funds: a figure representing the average length of maturity in the present money fund industry. The index shows nothing more than how popular long-term and short-term notes are at the moment.

If the maturity date is long it may mean money market fund managers are locking themselves into long maturities because they expect rates to drop; if the average maturity date is brief it means money market managers are seeking short-term funds because they expect the interest rates to rise. www.sec.gov/spotlight/money-market

certificate of deposit also known as CD: a receipt for a sum of money placed in the bank which earns interest and is insured by the Federal Deposit Insurance Corporation for up to $250,000 per individual.

CMA: abbr. Cash Management Account. The investor's money, which may come from stock dividends, real estate holdings or bond interest, is automatically placed by the investment firm in various interest earning liquid assets or in an interest earning checking account.

commercial banks also known as full service: nongovernmental banking institutions which lend short-term funds, provide credit cards, personal loans, foreign exchange, safe deposit boxes, investment management, accounts under trust, and every other conceivable function to private customers as well as to commercial groups for purposes such as financing businesses' needs for production, distribution, and sale of goods. The United States government's FDIC (Federal Deposit Insurance Corporation) covers up to $250,000 per depositor, per insured bank, for each account ownership category.

commercial paper: an IOU for large amounts of money (minimum of $100,000) issued by banks, businesses and investment firms. These short-term promissory notes are usually sold for a period of anywhere from twenty-four hours to 270 days. Investors in commercial papers tend to be other large companies or individuals with large sums of money who receive for these loans interest approximately equal to prime rate. The IOU usually has no collateral and is backed by the general reputation of the issuer.

credit union: The Federal Credit Union Act was passed by Congress in 1934 ". . . to make more available to people of small means credit for provident purposes through a national system of cooperative credit. . . ." This non-governmental financial institution's customers are members who own shares in the credit union and may receive dividends from the institution's earnings. Credit unions offer the same services as commercial banks and lend money at more favorable rates. Run by the National Credit Union Administration (NCUA), individual bank accounts are insured up to $250,000.

custodian bank: a bank charged with safekeeping assets.

debt instrument: another term for loans and the contract between the lender and borrower stating the debt agreement between them such as interest rate and maturity.

discount rate: the rate the Federal Reserve Bank charges its member banks for borrowing money. The rate is indicative of the banks' cost of funds.

Eurodollar Certificate of Deposit: the same concept as US CDs issued outside the United States by a foreign bank in US dollars. The liability varies because the CD is not issued by an American bank.

Eurodollar: deposits of US dollars in banks and other financial institutions in Europe. The Eurodollar market dates back to 1957. The decline in the use of sterling as an international currency was accompanied by an increased use of the dollar. Transactions take place outside the country whose currency is being dealt in, and the success of the market owes a great deal to the fact that it is outside the control of any national authority.

Euro Time deposit: a deposit in US dollars outside the United States in a foreign bank or an overseas branch of a US bank. It is non-negotiable and must be held for a set term to receive the interest in full.

FDIC: abbr. Federal Deposit Insurance Corporation. An independent agency in the federal government established to insure the deposits in all member banks.

Federal Reserve Bank: a national bank clearing system whereby each member bank keeps a certain percentage of its money on deposit at the local Federal Reserve Bank. The reserve is lent each day to banks that may be short of funds that day. The interest rate charged is known as the federal funds rate. As a rule the prime rate is usually higher by a few points than the federal funds rate.

401K: a retirement plan where contributions are automatically withdrawn from an employee's paycheck which also includes a reduction of the taxes on the contributed money. The employee may choose from a list of offerings how to invest the money. There are regulations about how much one may contribute annually and how and when one may withdraw the money.

International Monetary Fund: formed after the Great Depression to further stability in global financial markets. Nearly all countries are members and subsidize the IMF. The United States is the largest contributor, thus having the largest voting block and veto power for all calls. *See* real gold prices

IRA: abbr. Individual Retirement Account. The US Treasury allows a certain amount of yearly tax deferred investments from the top of one's salary to provide a secured nest egg for retirement. *See* Roth IRA

liquidity: ability to convert investments to cash with no or minimum penalty.

money market accounts: different from checking accounts in that money market accounts earn interest and a limited number of checks may be written monthly or electronically withdrawn.

money market certificate: a certificate for a small amount of private money, usually in the sum of $10,000, which is pooled to lend large sums of money to corporations at higher than savings account interest rates. These certificates require in most cases a six-month deposit and have severe financial penalty for early withdrawal.

money market fund: not to be confused with money market accounts. Organized like a mutual fund that invests in quality short-term debts.

money market instrument: investments in a type of debt vehicle such as short-term treasuries, CDs, mutual funds that invest in money market funds, and overnight call rate which refers to the rate banks charge each other when they borrow funds among themselves.

money market mutual fund: a type of mutual fund which invests in minimal risk debt securities. *See* mutual fund

money market rating services: supply ratings by statisticians who keep track of money market funds' credit risks, rate risks and market risks. The best-known services in the field are *Standard and Poor's, Moody's,* and *Fitch.*

money velocity: the speed with which money turns over. In a strong economy money frequently changes hands.

municipal discount notes: *see* municipal notes

no load: commission free; most money funds do not take a commission.

NOW accounts: abbr. negotiable order of withdrawal. Provide free checking accounts which require at all times a minimum deposit. In return the bank will pay the account-holder interest on the money in the account. If the account drops below the minimum, the bank imposes a service charge.

prime rate: *see* Index.

project notes: a fund of short-term projects often with a specific project written into the indenture specifying that the money must be used only for the specific project. These notes frequently offer higher interest than the prime rate. The US government from time to time issues such notes when involved with special housing development.

REPOs: abbr. repurchase agreements. Bonds, notes or CDs are sometimes sold by a bank or investment house to another investment house with the privilege of repurchase. The repurchase agreement may include accrued interest and/or repurchase at a few points above the original selling price. These transactions are short-term and fulfill the need for short-term liquidity without having to sell loan issues.

Roth: a retirement account into which one may place investments after having paid the taxes on the investments. Once in the Roth retirement account the investments may continue to grow and when withdrawn are tax-free. There are requirements as to how long the investment has to be in the account and at what age one may start to withdraw penalty-free. *See* IRA

SSC: abbr. small saver certificate. Used mainly by children and young adults because it has a small minimum balance requirements or no minimum while still paying an interest rate.

STIF: abbr. short-term investment fund. Offer liquid accounts allowing investors to add money or withdraw money while earning interest and are considered among the safest investments.

treasury securities: borrowings by the federal government from investors. *See* treasury bills, treasury notes, and US Savings Bond

DIAMONDS, GEMS, VALUABLE COINS, AND PRECIOUS METALS

about uncirculated: a choice coin that has hardly been circulated.

American Gem Society: is committed to protecting the consumer. It sets standards and awards titles to firms. It defines itself in part as a "trade association of retail jewelers, independent appraisers, suppliers, and selective industry members."
www.americangemsociety.org

American Numismatic Association: *see* coin grading services
www.money.org/about-ana

American Society of Appraisers: ASA describes itself as "the only professional appraisal organization accrediting professional appraisers from all six (6) appraisal disciplines." One of the disciplines are gems and jewelry.
www.appraisers.org

ASA LTD.: is a well-known investment company registered with the SEC, focused solely on precious metal and mining industry. Its securities are sold as closed end mutual funds.
See closed end
www.asaltd.com

assays certificate: a document of verification that the metal being purchased is pure and real. Gold and silver are considered precious metals.

blue white also known as color: a label for a diamond with no color except a bluish tinge which contributes to value.

brilliant: a diamond cut with fifty-eight facets, thirty-three above and twenty-five below the girdle.

brilliant coin: a gold or silver coin of exceptional luster.

certificate of deposit: a receipt of ownership of a certain quantity of gold bullion or coins. Historians consider these certificates forerunners of money. Today people may hold gold bullions or coins in a safe. There are banks who specialize in gold and silver sales and storage.

clarity: the degree to which a diamond is without flaw; contributes to its value. Gemologists use 10x magnification to identify and classify these clarity characteristics by size, type and position.

coin gradings: terms used to describe the general characteristics of coins. The condition of the coin is expressed numerically between one and seventy. Seventy denotes perfect condition. Trained experts look to see if designs and date are clear, and how worn the coin is.

www.money.org/about-ana

coin grading services: American Numismatic Association is a trusted and recognized resource for all particulars concerning coins.

www.money.org/tools

color: refers to diamonds. *See* blue white

COMEX: abbr. Commodity Exchange. Includes in its complex Chicago Mercantile Exchange, Chicago Board of Trade and New York Mercantile Exchange. Trades (among other commodities) gold and silver.

costume jewelry: jewelry containing imitations of gems and metals and materials of little value. Designed to wear to enhance fashion.

counter-cyclical metal: trends involving metals contrary to stock market trends, such as gold going down when the stock market goes up, and vice versa.

diamond: pure carbon, the hardest substance known to man; crystals found mostly in octahedron formation so rough they were not valued by the ancients until scientific cutting was developed. Considered by many as a hedge against inflation, wealth more easily portable than gold.

electronic metals: metals including antimony, germanium, indium, iridium and rhodium used in key laser components and other sophisticated technology.

Exchange Stabilization Fund: an agency within the US Treasury Department which has more than $1 billion at its disposal to use as it sees fit to stabilize currencies.

extremely fine: label for a coin in which practically all intricate details show.

fine: label for a coin acceptable to collectors.

fine weight: the total weight of the pure gold or silver in a metal, jewelry, or coin.

fineness: the proportion of pure gold or silver in coins, jewelry, or bullion expressed in parts per thousand.

first water: pure white diamond that is free of flaws, which contributes to its high value.

14 karat gold: the most commonly used gold for gem settings. It's composed of 58.3 percent gold and 41.7 percent alloy. 14k necklaces are popular because they are known to have nice color and a lasting durability.

gem: a cut and polished stone possessing durability and value; beautiful enough to use for jewelry.

gem coin (coin grading): flawless gold or silver coin.

gem material: any synthetic material that can be substituted for a real stone.

gem mineral: any mineral species which meets the qualifications of a gem and may thus be made into jewelry.

GIA: abbr. Gemological Institute of America. Known as the most reliable and exact source of diamond certificates in the world which include quality grading and assurance of diamond quality. www.gia.edu/gia-about. GIA is also known for its *Gem Encyclopedia* which offers a complete list and description of gemstones.

gold: the oldest precious metal; it does not rust, tarnish, scale or decay. 24 karat gold is pure gold. It is soft and bends easily and thus is not used for jewelry.

gold and silver dealers: those who buy and sell and sometimes store gold and silver in coins or bullion for clients; includes banks, brokerage houses, and coin dealers.

gold bar: a bar of gold; comes in sizes from ¼ ounce to 400 ounces.

gold bullion: bars of gold in various weights and usually stored in bank vaults; their value is controlled by market price.

gold bullion coins: coins that vary in size and fluctuate with gold market price.

gold coin: the value depends upon the amount of gold in the coin. Gold coins are easy to transport and store, and are considered a protection against the devaluation of money.

gold standard: gold as a monetary standard. Since gold is heavy to transport, nations who originally used gold as a monetary standard issued money. This money is actually considered as certificates of deposit for gold. The United States no longer uses the gold standard.

gross weight: the total weight of a gold or silver piece including its alloys.

ingot: any metal cast into a bar or other shape.

International Gemological Institute: lists among its services "operating 20 laboratory locations around the world grading finished jewelry, natural diamonds, lab-grown diamonds and gemstones—and 14 schools of gemology graduating thousands of new jewelry professionals each year." Because it assesses in its laboratories the value of gems it allows customers ready to invest in jewelry to know exactly what they are buying. www.igi.org/about-igi

International Gem Society: an informational and educational service which offers courses and facts online to all those interested in gemstones. www.gemsociety.org

junk silver: pre-1965 silver dimes, quarters and fifty-cent pieces. These silver coins contain 90 percent silver and are traded in bags. The price is determined by the current price of current silver bullion.

karat: in the United States, the degree of fineness of solid gold.

key coins: in a series coin collection, coins made popular by supply and demand; the most popular coins in a series.

light metals: metals such as beryllium, magnesium, titanium, and their various alloys which are not sensitive to light, heat or electronic impulses; vital in space structures because of their light weight combined with toughness. Some are mixed with the metal gold to strengthen it.

London Metal Exchange: marketplace that trades gold, silver, and other metals.

marking: the hallmark of an exchange approved refiner on jewelry or on a bar of gold or silver such as 14k gold or sterling silver or recognized names such as Tiffany or Cartier.

medallion: a gold coin which is not legal tender, often minted as a commemoration or to honor someone.

metal traders: professionals who make up the free market in metals. They trade in all the metals and are active in metal exchanges where the future of these metals are traded. Some traders are large firms which own metals as a hedge and which subsidize mines. *See* hedge

metals broker: an agent who buys on the market for a client for a commission and other fees such as storage, insurance, and assays costs. The broker negotiates each individual purchase with one or more metal traders for the best price.

mintage: the number of any one coin minted (manufactured).

Mohs Scale of Hardness: a universally used general standard of comparison in noting the hardness of a gem expressed by numbers from ten to one. A diamond, the hardest gem, is #10; talc, the softest, is #1.

natural placer gold: gold in its natural form as gold nuggets and dust.

numismatic coins: gold or silver coins minted long ago and now enjoying added value because of their rarity and historic value; often considered works of art. *See* American Numismatic Association

off-the-wall indicators: world and political occurrences that affect world gold and silver demand without having anything to do with supply and production.

pearl: a concretion composed of aragonite and calcium carbonate found in oysters and other mollusks. Valued by some in the highest rank of jewels although not as durable (hard) as crystalline gems. According to the Gemological Institute of America the value of pearls is determined by "7 factors: shape, size, colour, lustre, surface quality, nacre quality and matching."

physical: a term to denote a cash payment and/or to receive a hard product such as gold coins or gold and silver bullion as opposed to receiving a certificate or stock.

poor man's gold: a term for silver because it is less expensive than gold but in many ways more volatile in upswings and downswings, which by and large follow those of gold.

precious metals: gold, silver and platinum which are metals with special physical and chemical properties that enhance their value. Some buy them as a means of maintaining the value of their wealth, others for decorative materials. They also are used as industrial commodities.

precious stones: comparatively valuable gems such as diamonds, rubies, sapphires, emeralds and pearls.

premium: the cost above the metal value added to a gold coin; gold bullion coins have a relatively low premium.

Proof: coins struck for collectors; not for circulation. www.usmoneyreserve.com

real gold prices: commercial demand; annual average US dollar prices of gold as established in London afternoon fixings; deflated or inflated by the world consumer price index constructed by the International Monetary Fund. *See* International Monetary Fund

seigniorage: the difference between the cost of the metal plus minting expenses and the face value of the money coined.

sell off: a term used to denote that the price will go down because people are selling.

semiprecious stones: a term not welcomed by the jeweler because it refers to varieties other than diamond, ruby, sapphire, emerald, and pearl. A case in point is jade, which is not listed as precious, but considering its resale value, it should not be categorized as semiprecious either.

shekel: an ingot of gold or silver; varies according to the market. First used by the Babylonians about 2,000 B.C. Today known in Israel as the New Israeli Shekel.

silver: a metal with a high degree of luster and polish and the highest thermal and electric conductivity of any substance.

silver bar: a bar of silver available in sizes from 1 ounce to 1,000 ounces.

specific gravity: the density of a gem. The simplest way to measure this is to place the gem in a measured cup of water and measure the water it displaces.

stockpiling funds: stocks of strategic metals and precious metals kept to provide raw material for production at a future date. The participating investor expects a better than average return when demand increases.

strategic metal fund: similar to a mutual fund; has in its portfolio twenty or more strategic metals that are considered most attractive. Very few firms have such funds available.

strategic metals: metals used for defense including cobalt, platinum, molybdenum, iridium, iron, steel, nickel, lead, tin, and zinc.

strategic metals mutual fund: a fund which buys and sells strategic and other metals for profit.

The Silver Institute: a research-oriented institute made up of industrial consumers, producers, and dealers to the industry.

www.silverinstitute.org

troy ounce: about 10 percent heavier than our American ounce. The term Troy comes from its original use in the Middle Ages in Troyes, France and is still used today to calculate the weight of precious metals.

24 karat gold: purest form of gold.

uncirculated: label for a flawless coin (no bumps, perfect rim). Coins that never were in public circulation.

US gold coin: a coin from the gold standard days.

very fine: the label for a coin where some intricate detail shows.

warehouse receipt: the title to the metal purchased and stored in a warehouse; usually includes (separately) assays certificates and an insurance policy. The receipt is a negotiable instrument.

REAL ESTATE

absentee owner: one who owns property either for seasonal use or investment and may leave its management to others.

acceptance: a written and signed contract agreeing to certain terms and conditions of an offer.

accessory unit: a legal apartment within a private home or secondary house on the building lot created for rental or other lodging purposes which may not be sold separately.

act of God: *see* Index

age-life depreciation: the life expectancy of a real estate asset, assuming the property receives normal maintenance. It is calculated by evaluating all forms of depreciation maintained by the real asset divided by the total economic life of the real asset.

agent: an authorized person who represents and transacts business for another. In real estate an agent may act for another to sell, rent or buy to or from a third party. *See* exclusive right to sell contract

air rights: the rights to the use of the open space above a property providing that it complies with the zoning laws and the area's building codes.

amortization: *see* Index.

apartment house: three or more self-contained residential units in either a high-rise building or a sprawling garden complex complying with the residential laws. These laws may vary from state to state. Some buildings may have rentals for stores and other businesses.

appraisal: the application of analytical techniques to arrive at the value of a piece of real estate. Far from an exact science, appraisal involves the attempt to assemble pertinent data by methods of selective research in appropriate market areas based on past sales.

appreciation: an increase of the value in an owner's raw land, investment property or house.

arrears: payments due but unpaid; in real estate, usually refers to mortgage payments and/or a lien or property taxes.

assessed valuation: the value of real estate upon which taxes are calculated.

assignment: the transfer of title or interest in writing from one person or group of people to another. There may also be a legal transfer of mortgage (an assignment of mortgage) or of contract.

assignment of lease: a tenant's complete relinquishment of lease to another. Not to be confused with sublease, in which the leaseholder retains the lease and may even make a profit by renting the space at a higher sum than the lease stipulates.

assumption of mortgage: *see* Index

attachment: *see* Index

attractive nuisance: a hazardous condition maintained on one's premises because the owner does not recognize its danger. For example, a circus may have a caged lion on its property. However, if the cage is such that an unknowing child can actually reach in between the bars to touch the lion, the owner is maintaining a hazardous condition. The owner needs to add a fence or other railing to make it impossible for a child to touch the lion.

avigation easement: permission for aircraft to fly below a certain elevation. This is common for properties near or bordering airports.

backfill: earth that has been moved for such purpose as digging a foundation and is then returned to properly grade the property.

bad title: a title which because of its flaws, such as unpaid debts or building violations, may be unacceptable to the purchaser.

base rent: a fixed minimum guaranteed rent in a commercial property lease. Additions might for example include percentages of net profits of retail sales.

bench mark: when surveying land, the mark on a permanent object to and from which elevation and other points can be referred. When speaking financially in real estate the term refers to comparing investment property to other properties known for their value.

betterment: an improvement that increases the value of the land. The term must be distinguished from those that only maintain value. For example, the heater in Carol Smith's apartment house broke down. She could maintain the value of her building by having the heater repaired or she could buy a new heating unit thus making her building worth more.

blighted area: definition varies from state to state. In essence it defines an area that is unsafe, rundown, and/or neglected.

bog: wetlands.

bona fide: done in good faith, without fraud.

capital expenditure: an accounting or outlay representing improvement and additions which may be chargeable to property accounts.

capital gain: the profit gained by a sale of real estate after adjusted expenses. The amount of the selling price above the acquisition price.

capitalization method also known as income approach: an attempt to calculate net profit by deducting estimated normal expenses from the amount of income the property should bring.

capitalize: to put cash into a project.

carryover clause: a clause that safeguards the listing agent's full commission in the event that the property sells after the listing agreement has already expired. *See* holdover period

caveat emptor: "Let the buyer beware." Concept that one buys at one's own risk after having examined the property.

closing costs: the costs incurred individually to the buyer of a piece of property as well as to the seller. In part these include escrow fees, lawyers' fees, title insurance, documentary stamps on deed, recording the mortgage and other items depending on the state and specific needs.

closing day: the day the agreement of a real estate sale is consummated. The buyer signs the mortgage, and other necessary formalities are concluded; title and deed are transferred to the new owner.

cluster development: a plan where buildings are grouped close together in order to leave open space for common property which might offer amenities such as a children play area or an outdoor sitting area.

commercial acre: the portion of land of a commercial development that is left after a certain percent of the acreage has been appropriated for sidewalks, streets, etc.

commercial property: an income property zoned for such businesses as hotels, motels, office buildings, shopping centers, warehouses, apartment houses and parking lots. Not to be confused with industrial, agricultural, or residential zoning.

commission: the fee paid by the seller to a broker for transacting a sale. The fee is usually or should be decided upon before the agent begins his work. Brokers usually have minimum rates, but may be renegotiated before a bid is accepted if the sale is not as high as the original asking price. The broker may or may not agree to lower his commission.

common property: land for the use of the public at large, often including property belonging to another, such as oceanfront property.

community land trusts: this land is owned by a trust, making the purchase of only a house more affordable. There is a grant for a certain number of years the owners may stay on the land, usually ninety-nine years. When the owners are ready to sell, the trust buys the house back at an equity based on the trust's formula. cltweb.org/clt-directory

community property: property owned jointly by husband and wife. Though laws vary from state to state, the term refers mostly to property obtained during the marriage.

condemnation: the exercise of eminent domain; setting apart land by the government for a particular use or purpose such as highways, military reservations, or other public exigency. If the land is in the hands of private owners, the government has to recompense the value and loss to the owners either in money or exchange of land. www.law.cornell.edu/wex/eminent_domain

conditional contract: a contract stating that transfer of title is to take place when the conditions of the contract have been fulfilled. Until then the title remains in the seller's name. A common condition is that the contract can only be fulfilled if the buyer can obtain a mortgage.

condominium: individual ownership within a building. The ownership may be of an apartment or an office with a deed and title. The owner may do as he or she wishes with the area. It may be leased, mortgaged, bought, or sold. Taxes are paid independently by each owner. The common areas such as garden, halls, heating, plants, garage, etc., are owned jointly and costs are shared.

contract: the document containing the conditions of the sale and transference of title of real property, drawn up in a valid manner containing all essential points to make the transaction binding.

conversion: the act of changing the use of real property, such as changing rental apartments into condominiums, offices, or co-ops, or changing a large private home into a school.

conveyance: the act of transferring property from one person to another. A contract and a deed are each forms of conveyance. *See* contract and deed

cooperative brokers also known as co-brokers: when a listing agent allows other agents to show the property and collect a commission when a sale is completed. Co-brokering is a legal and common practice.

cooperative building: a building whose owners are stockholders in a corporation that owns the real estate. Each owner pays, depending on the size of his area, a fixed rate to cover operating costs, mortgage, and taxes. A cooperative may be owned in an office, apartment building, or industrial park. Not to be confused with co-ownership, which refers to two or more persons jointly owning an asset.

covenant: an agreement written into a deed stipulating certain acts and uses. Some may be restrictive, such as if a house should be built on a neighboring available lot it may only have a certain height.

deed: the legal document used on closing day to transfer real property from one owner to another. Contains an accurate description of the property being conveyed and is signed, witnessed, and carried out according to the laws of the particular state.

depreciation: the decline in value of property. Loss in market value may occur for many reasons; for example, deterioration of a neighborhood or an act of God. Appraisers define depreciation as the difference between present market value and replacement cost.

developer: a person who, for profit, puts land to its best use by the construction of improvements upon it. The land may be subdivided into homes, shopping centers, industrial parks, apartment houses or recreational facilities.

development property: 1) property already explored and known to be suitable for further development of such resources as oil, gas, precious metals, etc. Because a certain amount of risk is involved, and because the investment may be beneficial to the needs of the country, the federal government sometimes allows tax benefits to the investor. 2) land ready to be developed into homesites or commercial property.

devise: real property given as a gift in a last will and testament. The person who receives the gift is known as the devisee; the one who bequeaths the property is known as the devisor.

diluvium: a deposit of land produced by a flood.

earnest money: a sum of money given in good faith by one wishing to purchase a piece of property. Upon acceptance, it becomes a bilateral contract until the legal contract is drawn up. The money is held in escrow by a trustworthy person such as a lawyer, agent, a bank or a title company.

easement: a limited right to use another's property temporarily or permanently. Allowing the electric company to place a pole is permanent; permitting a neighbor to cross one's land until a road is built is temporary.

emblement: that which the lessor may take from the land after a lease expires; for instance, a tenant farmer whose lease is up may take the crop after it matures.

eminent domain: specifies the government's right to take private property to convert it into public use. The Fifth Amendment protects the property owners by particularizing that just compensation must take place.

encroachment: an intrusion upon the property of another without consent as, for example, a wall or fence that protrudes beyond its property line. If no one objects, it may be adjudged an implied easement. Encroachments may be delt with in any sale contract.

encumbrance: a legal right or interest in land that diminishes its value. It may be a pending legal action, change of zoning, easement rights, or liens. This does not prevent the owner from selling the land as long as a title search is done to reveal such encumbrances, and the buyer is willing to accept them.

escrow account: *see* Index

estate taxes: those federal and state taxes paid upon the transfer of property from the deceased to heir and legatees. State taxes vary and multiple state taxation may occur if the deceased had more than one domicile in more than one state.

eviction: the act of forcing a person out from a property. The most popular cause for eviction is typically for failing to pay rent or causing damage to the property. Legally time is given to the tenant to vacate the property. Other but less frequent reasons for eviction demands are tenants whose leases have expired but stay while continuing to pay the rent or a landlord who wants an apartment emptied for certain financial conveniences such as turning it into a co-op and decides to make the renter uncomfortable by not supplying such needs as hot water so that the renter will want to leave.

exclusive right to sell listing contract: a written agreement employing a broker for a specific time to the exclusion of all others. If another broker or the owner should sell the property in question during this time, the exclusive agent still gets a commission. *See* open listing and carryover clause.

exploratory property: property in which investments have been made in hopes that experts will discover a natural resource. Since no one knows for sure what the property contains until it is tested, such investments may be very risky.

fair housing act: housing free from discrimination based on sex, race, religion, color, national origin, mental health, or physical disability.
www.justice.gov/crt/fair-housing-act-1

federal public lands: lands under the auspices of the federal government and managed for the United States citizens. There are various types of public lands such as National Parks, National Wilderness Areas, National Forests, etc., which international visitors as well like to visit.
www.doi.gov/valuationservices/federal-lands-division

fee simple: complete and absolute ownership of land and buildings on it which makes it freely transferable and inheritable. Any limitations that exist do not result from the nature of the estate itself but are due to such controls as zoning, building codes, etc. It is the most common ownership in the United States.

firm price: a quoted selling price from which the owner will not deviate either by negotiating or accepting anything less.

first right to buy: the privilege given to a person to buy or lease real estate before anyone else; the right to meet any offer. Sometimes HOAs give first right to buy for a certain number of days to the owners in the building or complex.

freehold: an estate in real property without a time limitation; free and clear ownership. *See* fee simple

front footage: the measurement of property frontage. Property fronting a busy main street, a beach, or a park may be more valuable than property fronting a side street.

functional obsolescence: the end result of a building outliving its usefulness because of inadequate electric wiring, outmoded elevator, etc., so that it cannot compete with more modern facilities.

general public improvements: public improvement that benefits many property owners in an area but cannot be directly charged to property owners. Improvements may include sewers or power or telephone lines.

graduated rental lease also known as step-up lease: a lease having a rent which commences at a fixed rate and increases at set intervals.

ground lease: a lease of land alone exclusive of any buildings on the ground.

heavy industry: Zoning varies from State to State. All take into account that heavy industry may be noisy, cause pollution and have other undesirable aspects.
lev.co/blog/financing/industrial-zoning

hectare: still used today to measure large areas of land in the metric system. One hectare is equal to 100x100 meter square area.
www.unitconverters.net/area/hectare-to-acres.htm

high rise: a building higher than six stories.

high-water mark also known as mean high water and shoreline: the dividing line between public and private property. The shoreline is determined by the high wash of the waves or by the vegetation line.

HOA: abbr. homeowners association. A consortium in a condominium complex, planned community or other type of subdivision that makes and enforces rules for the properties and residents. Those who purchase properties within an HOA's jurisdiction become members and pay HOA fees.

holdover period: a clause in an exclusive listing which stipulates that the broker is protected for a specified time beyond the expiration date if someone who was shown the property when the listing was in force should later decide to buy the property.

homestead: a family home owned and occupied by husband, wife, or brother(s) or sister(s) protected by state laws against eviction by general creditors except in cases of a real estate tax lien or a mortgage lien directly involving the home.

HUD: an executive department of the US federal government, known as the United States Department of Housing and Urban Development which concerns itself with public housing, rental assistance, federally owned properties for sale and other housing issues.

improved land: land which has been enhanced and made either more livable by the addition of such amenities as roads, sewers, wells, buildings, or bridges, or fit for farming by the installation of an irrigation system and water lines.

inclusive rent also known as fixed, flat or gross lease: a rental arrangement that encompasses such charges as gas, electricity, heat, parking, etc.

income property: property purchased primarily for monetary return such as an apartment house or a shopping center.

incurable depreciation: property beyond repair or where remodeling would be uneconomical.

index lease: a lease that provides for adjustment of rent according to changes in a price index such as the consumer price index.

inspection by buyer: occurs after the seller has accepted the buyer's offer. If the buyer finds problems with the property, there may be renegotiations.

intrinsic value: what a seller is willing to accept and what a buyer is willing to pay. What we would say in daily terms as "the going price." Intrinsic value is also the price it would cost to replace a building on the property and/or what a similar piece of property would cost.

investment property: property bought for the sole purpose of providing income or bringing profit at some future date.

joint tenancy: ownership by two or more persons with rights of survivorship. Only one title exists. The death of one does not destroy the owning title; the survivor receives the decedent's share.

just compensation: a court-determined amount a person is to receive for the taking of his or her property. *See* eminent domain

land trust: a trust where real estate is the only asset. *See* trust

land use intensity: a series of density ratings regarding floor area, open space, living space, and recreation space. Zoning codes vary from area to area.

landlord: the owner of a leased premise.

lease: an agreement between a landlord and a lessor whereby the landlord grants the right of possession for a sum of rent and other obligations to the lessee (tenant), but retains the right to retake possession of the premises after the agreement has expired.

lease option: a lease containing a clause giving the tenant the right to purchase the property. There are many different and variable features to such leases; for example, some leases state that the rent may be deducted from the purchase price.

legal description: a description of a piece of property based on field notes of a surveyor or civil engineer and including lot, block, subdivision's government survey, and metes and bounds (terminal points and angles, distances and compass direction). Such descriptions are required by mortgagors, title companies, deeds and other legal instruments dealing with land.

leverage: the use of borrowed funds to buy real estate that will increase in value so that it can be sold, and the larger return from which will not only show a profit, but will also pay off the debt and other investment costs.

levy: to assess property and set the rate and the cap of taxation. The term is used by the Internal Revenue Service when it has a *levy permit* to seize property and/or other assets to pay a tax debt.

light and air: there are no natural rights to light and air, and a neighbor has a right to erect a structure obstructing light and air. Easements designating where a neighbor may and may not build can be obtained in writing. These legal easement possibilities vary from state to state.

listing contract: to register property for sale or rent with an agency; an agency's register of property available. In real estate parlance there are many kinds of agreements. *See* exclusive right

littoral land: land that borders a pooled or standing body of water, such as a lake, ocean, or sea.

maintenance fee: the cost levied against property owners to maintain a commonly owned complex which may include the cost of parking facilities, utilities, landscaping, and other benefits such as gyms and swimming pools. *See* HOA and condominium

management agreement: a contract between the owner of a residential or income property and the individual or firm that will manage the property. The contract includes fees, scope of responsibility such as for repairs, payment of expenses, and termination procedures. Some states require managers to be licensed.

marginal land: land that has a small prospect for profit because it has poor access, is too steep, and/or does not lend itself to industry, residential or agricultural purposes.

market value: the determination of what a piece of real property will sell for, arrived at following appraisal of similar sales in the area and allowing for condition, location, view and sufficient time to find a buyer.

master deed or lease: a condominium's principal deed or lease together with a declaration submitted according to state law when registering the complex.

mineral rights: the right to subsurface profits. These rights are not automatic and must be included in the deed when land is purchased.

mutual water company: a company organized by and for water users in a given district in order to have water at a reasonable rate. The stock is purchased by the users. Such companies are usually formed when a large new development is built which can't hook up to the nearest town's water because of distance or size.

National Association of Realtors: association which has over a million members of residential and commercial brokers as well as others involved with real estate such as appraisers and property managers. They have a code of ethics, provide counsel, important information and have conferences. *See* realtor www.nar.realtor/about-nar

net lease: a lease on which the lessee pays not only rent, but also maintenance and operating costs including taxes, insurance, utilities, and repairs. Such leases are popularly used by industries and commercial outfits. Landlords like them because they do not have the usual management problems.

net usable acre: the portion of a property suitable for building. Building may be limited not only by terrain such as wetlands and roadways, but also local zoning laws.

nominee agreement: one delegated to act in a limited sense for another party as a trustee. For example, if a person wishes to buy property or securities, the delegated may have his name titled on properties or securities while still leaving his customer as the legal owner.

notice of tax assessment: a document issued by the state or local taxing agency to the owner of real property specifying the assessed valuation of the property and how much of that value is taxable. As a rule the assessed value is not as high as the market value.

100 percent location: prime business property usually with a high traffic and pedestrian count; an area with highest rental prices.

open house: an appointed time when interested buyers may view a property for sale. When a broker holds an open house, the renters or owners usually vacate the property.

open listing: a listing given to all brokers in the area. The one who sells the house for the seller earns the commission. Should the homeowner find a buyer on his or her own no one gets a commission. *See* exclusive right to sell listing contract

over-improvement: a term to denote that when two adjacent properties are dissimilar the worth of the better property is lessened. For example, Mary and John Smith own a four-bedroom house with a swimming pool on a block where all the other houses are two-bedroom, two-family houses. Mary and John will not get as much for their house if they decide to sell as they would if the same house with a swimming pool was in a differently characterized block. Because of the nature of the neighborhood, the addition of the pool and the two bedrooms was an overimprovement of the property.

percentage lease: a lease used by rental businesses where the tenant pays a base rent plus percentages of the monthly or annual gross sales made on the premises. There are many types of percentage leases and they are especially popular with retail stores.

plat: a map of a town showing sections or subdivisions indicating boundaries of individual properties blocks, as well as public easements, dates and scales. In most cases these maps can be found in the town's tax assessor's office or city hall.

progress payments: payment to the builder of a condominium or house as the building proceeds. Final payments are made when the buyer is satisfied that the work is completed according to specifications. Such arrangements are usually made in conjunction with a lawyer and a lending institution.

property income: monies from rents after expenses have been paid.

proprietary lease: when buying a co-op property such as an apartment the buyer is purchasing shares in a corporation rather than real estate and is granted a proprietary lease for his/her unit.

raw land: land in its natural state.

real estate: the earth below, above and at level grade with or without structures, trees and water.

real estate option: to keep open an offer for a limited and agreed-upon time to buy or sell real property at a certain price. Such an agreement may give a developer time to check out zoning laws, or it may give a person wishing to buy a private house time to resolve financial questions.

real estate syndicate: consists of a group of people who have pooled their money to buy real property for the purpose of investment. Some participants may assume a passive role and only supply the capital, while others in the group may market and manage the property.

realtor: a member of state and local real estate boards affiliated with the National Association of Realtors. A realtor is a professional governed by the rules and regulations of the National Association of Realtors.

registrar: the person in charge of the records of all deeds, mortgages and other real estate titles.

REIT: abbr. Real Estate Investment Trust. Similar to an investment company, but concentrates its holdings in real estate investments, especially mortgages.

reliction: gradual recession of water from land, and therefore an increase of the land. Such uncovered land belongs to the owner of the property touching the border of the water.

rent: fixed-period payments made to the owner of a premise in return for occupancy with certain conditions and agreements.

rent control: regulations by state and local governmental agencies restricting the amount of rent that landlords can charge their tenants. Rent control is only needed when there is an imbalance of supply and demand.

rental pool: an agreement by participating owners of condominiums to have their units available for rental with a rental agent, and to share in the profits and losses of all rental apartments in the pool as agreed upon. Such pools are especially popular in resort areas where the owners only use their condominiums as a second home.

right of way: a privilege acquired by either usage or contract to pass over another's property. Tom Field owned a farm of several hundred acres, and the railroad had a right of way to build tracks on part of his property. Mary Smith bought raw land several hundred yards from the road; her deed included an easement that she may not be cut off from the road.

riparian: literally means riverbank and refers to the rights and obligations of ownership of land adjacent to or abutting on streams. Some riparian rights may be swimming, boating, fishing, etc., open to all. Laws may vary from state to state.

royalty: the sum paid to owners of realty for the privilege of extracting its natural resources such as oil, gas, timber, gravel, or builder's sand.

run with the land: covenants such as easements which bind successive owners of a property.

sale-leaseback: a financing device whereby a developer or an owner of a home sells his or her home to an investor (to get cash) and then leases it back under a long-term net lease. There are many variations and tax implications to this type of transaction which must be thoroughly studied before entering into such an arrangement.

security deposit: money deposited, usually one month's rent, by or for the tenant with the landlord to protect the landlord against damages, failure to pay rent, and other problems. State laws vary on the interpretation of its uses and each lease should state the interpretation. For example, some security deposits are deposited in an interest-paying account and the interest is paid to the tenant. As a rule if the property is in good condition when the renter moves out the security deposit is returned.

separate property: property held individually, as opposed to community property. *See* joint tenancy

special assessment: taxes levied for the cost of specific local improvements such as sewers, irrigation, drainage, and streets, to be paid only by those owners who will benefit by it. Co-ops and condominiums may also have special assessments added onto their HOA fees to fix roofs, windows, and common facilities such as a fitness center or swimming pool.

spot survey: a quick visual property survey done without the use of surveying tools and only pointing out location, size, and the type of buildings located on the lot.

spot zoning: a variance in the zoning law to permit change in a small area in a generally larger area, such as a two-family house in an area zoned only for single houses. Spot zoning can be very controversial and laws vary from state to state.

squatter rights: living on land or in a building for a number of years without being evicted thus demanding to obtain rights to land or building when occupation is deemed untitled. State laws vary as to what amount of time (five, seven, twenty years) land must be occupied by the squatter(s).
learn.eforms.com/real-estate/squatters-rights

subdivision: any land divided into two or more lots for the purpose of sale; not to be confused with master plan or zoning. Regulations for subdivisions vary from state to state.

subject to mortgage: *see* conditional contract

sublease: permission by a leaseholder for a second or third party to occupy rented premises for the whole term or part of it, usually for a higher price than the lessee is paying the landlord. Some leases contain clauses prohibiting subletting. The lessee always pays the landlord and collects directly from the second and/or third party.

survey: when professional surveyors verify on-site measurement of lot lines, dimensions and positions of house or houses in a lot including encroachment or easement from adjacent properties and more.

syndicate: *see* Index.

tax assessment: when a government assessor determines the value of the real estate to determine the amount of taxes to be

paid. Considerations include location, construction type, its use (such as agriculture or residential), vacant land and more factors. The owner may request a reassessment.
www.irs.gov/irm/part35/irm_35-009-002

tenant: the one who holds a lease.

tenancy in common: when one owner dies the deceased share goes to the heir(s) if there is no will, as state law dictates.

tideland: land between high and low tides that is covered and uncovered by the ebb and flow of the tides.

time sharing: the purchase or lease by multiple purchasers of a partial interest in a property (usually in a resort), giving them the right to use the facility for a fixed or variable time period each year. The cost is prorated among the owners.

title: lawful ownership to the property in question.

title insurance: protection for the property-owner against a forged deed or anything else that may have happened in the past to make the title worthless.

title search: an examination of the public records to trace the successive titles to the specific property up to the present owner. The search should prove the title to be marketable, clear and not defective in any way. *See* title insurance

trust: real estate, securities, and other financial holdings held and administered for the benefit of another.

turnover of working capital: in a given period, income in dollars produced by each dollar of net working capital; calculated when buying raw land or other real estate for investment.

undivided interest also known as undivided right: rights of joint owners in a property that cannot be separated from the other owners; tenants in common also have rights that cannot be separated from the other tenants.

undulating land: gentle sloping property; elevation changes of 3–8 percent.

unearned increment: an increase in property value not because of the owner's skill or efforts, but rather because of population increase, new zoning laws, the unexpected building of a nearby airport, etc.

unencumbered property: real property free and clear of mortgages, liens and assessment of any kind.

usufruct: the right to enjoy and profit from a particular property even though one does not own it. This right is as a rule for a limited time. An example is Joe Smith owns a farm. He becomes unexpectedly infirm. His son, Sam, and Sam's family move into Joe's home, run the farm and use the profits to support Sam's family, as well as send his daughter to college. Sam does not have the right to damage, destroy, sell or give away the farm.

variance: an exception made to the zoning laws. Permission must be obtained from the court. For example, a variance might be made in a residential area to permit a small, much-needed grocery store.

wasteland: land unfit for cultivation or development such as swamp or desert.

LOANS AND MORTGAGES

add-on interest: a method used in installment loans in which the interest is added to the principal at the outset of the loan. The borrower receives only the principal requested, which includes the larger sum of principal plus interest.

advice: *see* Index

amortization: a principal payment in reduction of a debt. The most common is a fully amortized loan, which is the gradual payment of the mortgage in periodic amounts until the total amount including interest is paid off. Amortization tables are available which show how much of the monthly payment is interest and how much principal. As the loan becomes smaller, the principal part of payment becomes larger, and the interest smaller.

annual percentage rate (APR): the cost of a loan figured on the amount of credit advanced as well as the amount of time the money is used.

arrears: behind either in paying a debt or taxes, or in work such as construction that is overdue and incomplete.

assets: possessions that have monetary value.

attachment: taking a debtor's property into collateral custody.

balance: amount of loan left to pay off.

balloon payment: *see* list under mortgage

balloon mortgage: *see* list under mortgage

bankruptcy: inability to pay one's obligations so that creditors acting through the federal court and its trustees may seize available assets.

business loan: usually short-term credit or money loan so that inventory purchases may be made, equipment purchased, or short-term money needs met. *See* capital

carrying charges: 1) the cost of carrying a debt; the fee asked by a store or other lender such as a credit card company for the privilege of charging goods beyond the bill's usual due date (loans); 2) costs incurred in owning property up to the time the development of the property is completed; this includes taxes and interest on loans (mortgages).

character: moral risk involved in negotiating credit or a partnership. Considered are: reputation for business honesty, habits such as gambling, promptness in paying obligations, standing in community, reputation of business associates, as well as business record which includes successes, bankruptcies, and failures. Also considered are fire record, police record, civil court record, and general business ethics such as honoring contracts, employing unfair competition, or circulation of false rumors.

charge-off: a loan declared as a loss because it cannot be collected.

chattel mortgage: a term for personal, movable property such as automobiles, furniture, and appliances; can be put up as security in a loan and be used as payment of a bad debt.

closed mortgage: *see* list under mortgage

collateral: any asset such as securities, real estate, vehicles, personal property, or life insurance used as a pledge for a loan.

commitment fee: *see* drop dead fee

consolidation loan: a new loan taken out to combine several debts so that only one large debt has to be paid off.

consumer credit: personal loans to individuals and families for personal use such as vacations or purchases, as opposed to loans for business or investment purposes.

cosigner: a jointly guaranteed loan of which only one signer has the use of the money. *See* hypothecation

credit card: a device which upon presentation obtains credit for the holder of the card; according to the US Congress, "'credit card' means any card, plate, coupon book, or other single credit device existing for the purpose of being used from time to time upon presentation to obtain money, property, labor or services on credit."
www.consumerfinance.gov/rules-policy/regulations/1002/ 2/#j

credit information: data obtained from reliable sources to evaluate credit worthiness. There are numerous credit bureaus, the majority of which belong to the National Association Of Credit Management and whose members exchange credit information with each other. The association will provide a summary of all others' experiences with the account in question without revealing individual tradespeople's names.
www.usa.gov/credit-reports
nacm.org

credit investigator: someone who works for a bank, mercantile agency, commercial paper house, or business firm examining the information given by applicants seeking loans and credit. The investigators' sources of information may come from credit files, banks, stores, and credit interchange bureaus as well as personal interviews.

credit line: the amount of credit a bank, lending institution, or trade firm will extend to a customer.

creditor: according to law, someone who regularly extends or arranges for credit which is repayable by agreement for which payment of a finance charge may be required.

deadbeat: slang for a poor credit risk.

deed of trust: a deed to real property given by a borrower as collateral for a debt. A third person (trustee) holds the instrument of ownership for the lender as well as the borrower. If the debt is not paid off, the trustee may sell the property at a public sale; this procedure varies from state to state.

default: the failure to comply with conditions such as payments due in a deed of trust, mortgage, or promissory note.

delinquent: past due; usually after a certain amount of grace period days as in a loan payment. *See* grace period

drop dead fee also known as commitment fee: a kill fee to be paid when a borrower asks banks and other lenders to rapidly organize large sums of funds (in denominations of hundred thousands, millions and even billions) and then does not after all borrow the money. The borrower of such large sums is usually a corporation.

due date: the date an installment payment must be made, or the date the final payment is made on a loan.

Equal Credit Opportunity Act also known as Title VII to the Truth in Lending Act: legislation passed in 1975 by the US Congress making it unlawful for any creditor to discriminate against any applicant on the basis of sex, age, race, color, public assistance or marital status with respect to credit transactions.

www.justice.gov/crt/equal-credit-opportunity-act-3

escrow account: an account set up by the lender of a mortgage into which the mortgage borrower pays monthly a sum of money together with his mortgage payment to cover property related expenses such as real estate taxes. *See* RESPA

Fair Credit Reporting Act also known as Consumer Credit Protection Act: legislation that regulates the purpose for which a consumer reporting agency may provide a consumer report and limits what may be contained in it. If a person is denied credit or employment on the basis of a reporting agency's report, the person must be informed of this and given the name of the credit agency. If the consumer feels cheated, the act provides recourse whereby the consumer can defend him or herself.

Fannie Mae and Freddie Mac: abbrs. Federal National Mortgage Association and Federal Home Loan Mortgage Association. Do not offer mortgages nor lend money. Fannie Mae and Freddie Mac purchase under the auspices of the federal government mortgage loans already made by lenders which then enables the lenders to have the cash flow to provide further mortgage loans.
www.fhfa.gov/about-fannie-mae-freddie-mac

Federal Land Bank System: a government agency which makes available long-term mortgages to farmers, enabling them to own their own farms. This agency is the largest holder of farm mortgages in the world.
www.fca.gov

finance charges: the full charges of a loan including not only interest cost but also fees, service charges, points, and investigation costs.

finance company: a state-regulated, licensed and bonded consumer loan company.

financial adviser: an expert who advises individuals or families on all their holdings, investments, mortgages, student loans and sometimes personal budgeting, accounting, estate planning, and taxes.

flat rate on unpaid balance: a rate set on a daily or monthly basis for unpaid bills, used mainly by all types of consumer stores and credit card issuers.

forced sale: the sale of property by an owner under duress; usually to satisfy unpaid taxes or liens.

foreclosure: a legal action to end all rights and possession of the mortgagor because of a default in the terms of the mortgage by the mortgagor; the property then becomes the possession of the mortgagee or guarantor. Laws vary from state to state. In general if there are excess funds left after the liens and expenses have been paid off a motion filed with the clerk at the court who issued the order of sale may be filed to allocate the remaining balance of the funds to the one who defaulted on the loan.

foreign correspondent: a bank in a foreign country acting and maintaining money for a domestic bank.

garnishment: a legal process by which a portion of the wages or salary of a debtor may be withheld by an employer for payment of debts.

grace period: the short time within which a past-due debt such as a mortgage may still be paid without penalty or default. Credit cards never have grace periods.

guarantor: one who pledges to pay a debt for another if necessary.

hangout: a long-term loan that exceeds the term of a lease for the same property. For example, John Smith built a factory for Mass Bakery Co., which signed a lease for ten years. John Smith's mortgage was for fifteen years with the stipulation that John Smith was to pay the balance of the loan if Mass Bakery did not renew its lease. *See* balloon mortgage

hypothecation: the pledge of property as security for a debt without giving up possession of it. A common example is giving a car as security while continuing to drive it. If the borrower does not meet the terms of the loan, the lender can seize it.

installment loan: a loan paid back in regular monthly amounts over a specified time.

installment plan: a method of buying merchandise on extended credit whereby interest is added onto the unpaid principal and a contract is signed outlining the cost to borrow and how much is to be paid monthly. Usually the merchandise stays in the seller's name until it is paid off.

interest rate: 1) simple: the cost of borrowing money; percentage charged on a principal sum of money to pay for borrowing that principal amount; 2) compound: interest calculated upon the principal plus old interest due; 3) discount: interest paid in advance. For example, 10 percent discount interest results in a $1,000 loan owed but only $900 given to the borrower.

late charge: the penalty for failure to pay a regular mortgage, other loan installment, HOA fees or rental.

letter of credit: a letter by a bank on behalf of its client authorizing another bank to make payments or accept drafts when the client has complied with all stipulations in the letter. The client guarantees payment to the bank issuing credit. For example, Carol Martin has a boutique in Cleveland and she needs to go on a buying trip to Italy. Her home bank knows that the boutique can afford to buy $25,000 worth of new merchandise, and issues a letter of credit for that sum on behalf of Carol Martin to their correspondent bank in Italy. The bank in Italy will pay the wholesaler (also known as the beneficiary or fourth party) within the specified amount once Ms. Martin presents her bills to the Italian bank.

lien: a claim on property until a debt is discharged.

loan assignment: transfer of a claim, right, or property of a borrower to a trusted person who then is in charge of whatever has been transferred.

loan shark: unlicensed lender who charges much higher rates than licensed lending institutions, and will sometimes only accept full payment so that the high rates may be charged on the full amount right to the last day.

loan-to-value ratio: the ratio of a mortgage loan to the property's appraised value or its sale price (whichever is lower) and depending on the lending institution's policy.

luxury assets: any items such as valuable jewelry, boats or vacation homes not needed for income or living necessities, but which may be used as collateral as well as have a value when liquidated.

maturity: the date a mortgage note becomes due or the date the final payment causes it to expire. *See* balloon payment and balloon mortgage

mortgage: a long-term recorded note securing the debt that provides cash with which to buy real property or refinance mortgaged property. Upon full payment, the note will be canceled. The property is always in the name of the mortgagor and not the lender. The property legally described is the lender's security in case of default, at which time the property may be sold and the debt satisfied with any additional money realized from the sale going to the mortgagor providing there are no other debts.

There are many different types of mortgages, among which are the following:

amortized mortgage: debt that is paid off in equal amounts periodically over a predetermined span of time until the total amount, along with interest (if any) has been completely satisfied. *See* amortization

ARM: abbr. adjustable rate mortgage. The interest rate of the loan is not fixed but after a determined time period changes then based on the current market. *See* amortization and variable amortization mortgage

assumption of mortgage also known as assumable mortgage: the taking on of complete responsibility for an existing mortgage by the purchaser of a property, thus releasing the original mortgagor.

balloon mortgage: specified and periodic installments of principal and interest that do not fully amortize the loan. The final balance is due in a lump sum at a specified date in the future.

blanket mortgage: a mortgage covering more than one piece of property.

buy down mortgage: the agreement by someone other than the mortgage holder—such as the builder of a house or a developer—to pay part of the interest for the first few years of the loan. The builder can afford to do this by including the "cost" of his share of the loan in the sale price of the house. A builder may offer the arrangement as an incentive in order to sell houses that would otherwise be slow moving due to market conditions.

closed mortgage: a mortgage where no further advances are provided by the lender.

condominium spot loan: allows the Federal Housing Administration to fund loans in an association, without the project having to obtain FHA certification.
www.hud.gov/program_offices/cio
www.hud.gov/sites/documents/41502HBHSGH.
DOC

Federal Housing Finance Agency (FHA) mortgage: a mortgage provided by a lending institution that obtains insurance from FHA, a federal agency; the mortgagor pays FHA an annual insurance premium against default.

www.fhfa.gov

first mortgage also known as first loan and first lien: the mortgage that is superior, takes precedent to any other in case of default. It will be the first mortgage debt paid.

fixed rate mortgage: a mortgage in which the interest rate stays the same for the life of the loan.

floating rate mortgage also known as variable rate mortgage: a loan for which the interest rate is not fixed, but moves up or down on the basis of indexes such as prime rate or treasury bills.

general mortgage: see blanket mortgage

graduated mortgage payment (GPM) also known as flexible rate mortgage: conceived originally by the Department of Housing and Urban Development but used today by other lending institutions, the GPM provides for below-market payments during the early years; the differential is added to the principal of the mortgage, and at a specified date, mortgage payments are increased to the then current market rate.

hard money mortgage: rather than considering the assets of the borrower, the lender looks at the worth of the investment the borrower wishes to buy and uses that investment as collateral.

junior mortgage also known as second mortgage: any mortgage such as a second mortgage subordinate in lien priority to a prior existing mortgage on the same property. John Smith has a mortgage on his house. He takes out a second mortgage. Should John default, his house will be sold. The cash from the sale will be used to pay off the first mortgage, and only what is left will be used to satisfy the second mortgage.

level payment mortgage: a mortgage repaid in equal periodic payments. *See* amortization

micro lender: see Index

open mortgage: a loan that may be repaid in full anytime without penalty.

open-end mortgage: a mortgage that secures not only the original note and debt to buy the property, but any additional advance the mortgagee may choose to make in the future for additions such as a playroom, a garage, etc. The costs of executing a new mortgage are thus avoided.

owner carry back: a mortgage taken back by the seller to be paid off by the buyer as part of the purchase price.

package mortgage: a loan that finances not only the purchase of a house, but also personal items such as specified large appliances.

purchase money mortgage: the seller of the real estate issues the mortgage the buyer needs to buy the property. If the buyer does not fulfill the obligations, the real estate in question reverts to the seller.

reverse mortgage loan: a loan sought mostly by older people who own their homes and wish to increase their retirement incomes. A new mortgage loan is taken out and given in monthly installments by the lender to the mortgagee over a period of years. Each payment is added to the unpaid principal amount. There are varieties to reverse mortgages. A lump sum may be given, or to ease monthly expenses, if there are monthly payments of mortgages left these may be paid off. Settlement of the loan is made when the estate of the family sells the house or when the owner of the house moves out.

rollover mortgage: one that replaces an existing mortgage and is "rolled over" for additional financing.

SAM: abbr. Shared Appreciation Mortgage. The borrower obtains the mortgage at a favorable interest rate and agrees, in exchange, to share the profits with the lender when the house is sold. If the house is not sold within a given time, the lender may refinance the outstanding principal at current interest rates.

split financing: a practice used by developers and investors whereby financing for land and improvements is arranged separately; allows a greater amount of money for a longer period.

spreader agreement: the extension of a mortgage lien to encompass other property owned by the borrower in order to give the lender greater security.

standing mortgage: an interest-only mortgage; principal is paid off at maturity. Not to be confused with balloon mortgage.

straight mortgage: a loan in which only interest payments are made periodically with the entire principal amount becoming due at maturity.

subsidized mortgage: a monetary grant by the federal government as well as guarantees by the government to facilitate mortgage arrangements for a necessary real estate project.

VA mortgage: a guaranteed loan made to an eligible veteran for the purchase or construction of a home with a small down payment or none at all.

variable amortization mortgage: a loan in which the principal does not initially have to be amortized or may be stepped up or down during the loan term. The rate of interest on the unpaid principal remains the same, while the amount of interest that must be paid will differ as the outstanding principal is reduced.

wrap-around mortgage: the combination of an original mortgage (retained usually because of a lower interest rate) and an additional mortgage (usually at a higher interest rate), becoming the junior mortgage. (*see* junior mortgage.) The entire loan (both mortgages) is treated as a single loan.

mortgage lien: a recorded instrument encumbering the property, and thus securing the underlying debt obligation. Because the lien is recorded, it receives priority over other obligations, provided it is a first lien. *See* junior mortgage

overdraft loan: overdraft on a checking account; allowed by certain banks with special arrangements. The overdraft is treated as a loan.

personal loan also known as signature loan: a loan secured or unsecured by an individual who may have a cosigner. *See* cosigner

personal security also known as personal guarantee: guarantor for another person's debt. While the financial worth of the guarantor is taken into consideration, there is no specific pledge of collateral.

plastic money: a term for credit or debit card.

points also known as discount points: percentages of the face of the loan; for instance, 2½ points on a $100,000 mortgage would be 2,500 payable to the lender on the closing of the loan.

prepayment penalty: a charge by the lender when a mortgage is repaid before maturity; a means to recoup a portion of interest that the lender had planned to earn when the loan was made. Many people seeking a mortgage try to avoid such a clause.

prepayment privilege: the right to pay off without penalty a part or all of a mortgage.

prime rate: the lending rate charged for loans which are considered as less risky; loans to those customers who are considered as the bank's prime clients. Rates higher than prime rate have "added premium" for risk.

www.federalreserve.gov/supervisionreg.htm

principal: the money amount exclusive of interest; the money amount upon which interest is charged.

private mortgage insurance: a special form of insurance whereby a private insurance company guarantees the loan and thereby permits the lender to issue a much higher mortgage, in some cases as high as 100 percent of the purchase price. It is the same service as that of the Federal Housing Agency, except the insurance is provided by private firms.

www.consumerfinance.gov

promissory note: literally a promise by the borrower to repay, according to specified terms, the amount borrowed plus any other charges, fees, and interest.

quit claim deed: a release of deed which releases whatever interest the grantor has in the property. Usually used between two trusting parties in real estate transactions.

rebate: the portion of the interest rate returned to the borrower when a loan is paid off early.

refinance: to obtain a loan to pay off another loan. This is done for several reasons, one of which is to generate additional capital to buy more property. Or, when interest on a particular mortgage is higher than the present rate, it is prudent to pay off the mortgage and arrange for a new one at the current rate.

release clause: a clause found in promissory notes and mortgages usually involving raw land or development property. As a stipulated portion is paid off, a designated amount of land is released so that the property in question may be sold or released from the collateral.

repossession: the act of taking back goods purchased on the installment plan because the buyer has fallen behind in the periodic payments. *See* installment loan

RESPA: abbr. Real Estate Procedures Act. All servicers of home loans such as mortgage must as required by the Federal Reserve Board disclose to borrowers all pertinent information regarding the real estate loan settlement process. The act also prohibits such strategies as kickbacks and has limitations on the use of escrow accounts. *See* escrow accounts

www.fedsearch.org/board_public/search?text=respa&Search

revolving account: an agreement with a store as to the maximum amount one can owe at any time; interest is charged for the credit. Generally this loan of credit can be used and paid off as needed.

right of rescission also known as "cooling-off" period: a provision of federal and some state laws allowing a purchaser to cancel a contract to purchase within a given time; this law was passed to help those who may have given in to high sales pressures when they really could not afford and did not wish to purchase the item.

satisfaction of mortgage: a certificate stating that a mortgage has been paid in full; must be recorded in order to be discharged of record.

secured loan: a loan secured by securities, passbook, life insurance or goods such as a car which can become the property of the lender in case of default. Such loans may charge a lower interest because of their excellent security.

security: an asset given as a pledge of repayment of a loan in case of default.

service charge: the fee apart from the interest paid on a loan.

simple annual interest: interest computed on the original principal and paid at the end of a year's use of the money.

single payment loan: a loan paid back in one lump sum; may be 1) a demand loan paid at the request of the lender, or 2) a time loan with a set date of repayment for the whole amount specified.

Small Business Administration loan: an investment, SBA loans are those funds lent to small businesses by banks and guaranteed by the US government.

soft money: a term to denote carrying charges.

special lien: a charge against a specific property or parcel of land such as a mortgage lien. A general lien is a charge against all the property of the debtor.

subordination agreement: an agreement by a prior mortgagee to become the junior mortgagee so that another existing or anticipated lien may be taken on. Such agreements are frequently used in development projects where a bank or other lending institution may refuse to lend money for construction unless it has the first mortgage position or in a refinance of a first mortgage.

tax lien: a lien against collateral for taxes due.

term loan: any loan with a maturity of over one year.

term of the loan: the length of the loan in months, days, or years.

time contract: an agreement stipulating periodic payments calculated to clear the debt by a specified maturity date.

tip: abbr. total interest payment. The mortgage contract has a disclosure page which states how much interest the borrower will pay over the lifetime of the mortgage loan.
www.consumerfinance.gov

Truth In Lending Act: a federal law regulating credit and protecting the consumer; the law requires that those seeking consumer credit be given clear, meaningful information about its cost; regulates certain credit advertising, certain credit transactions involving real estate, and issuance of credit cards with limitations on the cardholder's liability for unauthorized use; designed to assist consumers in resolving credit billing disputes.

usury: the practice of charging an excessive amount of interest; charging more interest than the legal rate. Each state has a maximum usury rate that may be legally charged.

warranty deed: a document that proves who has the title to a property by stating all the legal details.

INSURANCE

accelerated option: a provision in a life insurance policy whereby the policyholder may use the policy's cash value and accumulated dividends to pay up the policy sooner than normal.

accidental death and dismemberment: a rule added as a rider to a life insurance policy. *See* rider

accommodation line: insurance business accepted by an insurance company from an agent that would have been rejected under normal circumstances but which is taken because of the agent's or customer's overall large account.

act of God: an occurrence such as a flood, hurricane, earthquake, tornado or blizzard; not created by or under the control of human beings.

actual cash value (ACV): a term used in the settlement of damage to personal items and property; the value of an item equal to the original cost minus depreciation.

actuary: a specialist trained in statistics and accounting who computes statistical tables relating to insurance; also computes premiums to be charged based upon the actual number of paid claims in a given time plus the insurance company's operating costs.

adjuster: a person who investigates a claim so that the claim will be settled by the insurance company; the adjuster may represent the insurance company or the policyholder.

age change: the date on which, for insurance purposes, a person's age changes are noted. Such a date is important in life and health insurance.

agency: person(s) known as agent(s) acting as an intermediary between insurance companies and the public. A direct agency represents only one insurance company and may be staffed by the insurance company; an independent agency represents many insurance companies.

aggregate limit also known as excess of loss reinsurance or stop loss reinsurance: a predetermined dollar amount during a specific period, usually twelve months, over which an insurance company is not liable; the maximum amount may be determined by a percentage of the company's premiums (loss ratio) for that period.

agreed amount policy: predetermined value of the insured item (rather than at the time of a claim).

aleatory contract: a contract depending on uncertain events such as accident, death, or natural disaster, and in which both parties realize that one party may obtain far greater value under the agreement than the other.

all risk: coverage provided for all types of physical damage except those specifically excluded. Gradual deterioration from vermin, rust, etc., is usually excluded.

ancillary benefits: benefits for miscellaneous hospital charges. After surgery there may be ancillary needs such as pain killers, physical therapy or medical massages.

annual renewable term: life insurance that may be renewed at the end of each year. The right to renew may extend to ten or more years and the face value of the policy stays level, although the cost may increase with age.

annual statement: the required annual report of an insurance company to the state insurance department showing assets, liabilities, receipts and disbursements, etc.

annuity: *see* Index

apportionment: the proportionate method of dividing the average (cost) when two or more companies cover the same loss.

appraisal: a written opinion of an item by an impartial expert which includes a description and dollar value.

APS: abbr. Attending Physician's Statement. The form filled out by doctors who have treated the proposed insured so that the insurance agent can prepare life, dis ability, or health insurance.

assigned risk: a risk not acceptable to insurers and therefore assigned to insurers in a pool. Each participating company accepts its share of these risks.

assignment: life, property, or disability insurance assigned to another person; can be done in two ways: collateral, which means that the assignee has only the rights of the policy to protect his or her interest, and absolute, which means the assignee has all the same rights as the original owner. The most common use is as collateral to protect mortgages on real property.

assurance: the British word for insurance.

attractive nuisance: *see* Index.

authorization also known as power of attorney or attorney in fact: an insurance term giving written permission to: 1) permit a company to inspect financial, medical, and moral records to determine eligibility for insurance, and 2) negotiate coverage rates to be charged on an insured's behalf.

auditable policy: a policy which may be audited to see if the insured overpaid or underpaid the premium and if need be the amount can be rectified. This usually involves commercial establishments where liability, payroll and other business factors are of importance.

average rate or risk: a single insurance such as fire insurance for two or more business locations where inventory may flow back and forth.

beneficiary: the person to whom proceeds from an annuity or life insurance are payable. This term is carefully qualified in an insurance policy stating whether it is revocable, irrevocable, and whether there is a secondary beneficiary.

benefit: depending on conditions in an insurance contract, the money paid out to the recipient. There are many kinds of benefits in insurance parlance.

benefit period: the length of time benefits will be paid for any one accident, illness, or hospital stay.

Best's Insurance Reports: a publication providing pertinent statistics, financial reports, and other information on all insurance companies doing business in the United States.

binder: a receipt given to a purchaser of insurance containing a new policy or new policyholder's terms which insures the policyholder until the actual policy is issued.

blanket insurance: insurance that covers more than one building, person, etc., in one policy.

broker: an agent who represents the buyer of insurance and may buy policies from more than one company.

bundling premiums: most insurance companies will give a discount to those who purchase more than one policy or all their insurance needs from their company. *See* premiums

cancellation: the termination of a policy either by the policyholder or the insurance company before the end of its contract period.

carrier: an insurer or insurance company.

cash refund annuity: those installments still unpaid at the death of the annuitant paid to a designated beneficiary in one lump sum.

cash surrender value also known as cashing in: the monetary value of a life insurance policy when it is terminated by the policyholder during his or her lifetime.

cash value: the value of a whole life insurance policy against which one may borrow at a specific rate of interest stated in the contract.

casualty insurance: insurance against loss due to legal liability to a third person; has many subtitles such as auto, storekeeper, or fire when tenant is legally responsible.

catastrophe: a severe and extreme loss such as of life or property; a special class of insurance. *See* liability

cede: to transfer to a reinsurer all or part of the insurance written by the relinquishing company because the cost is beyond the company's means. See reinsurance

certificate of insurance: in group or individual insurance, a document stating the period within which one is insured, as well as limitations and coverage.

claim: following a loss, the request for reimbursement under an insurance contract as well as the final settlement.

clause: in an insurance policy, a section or paragraph that explains, defines, or clarifies the conditions of coverage.

CLU: abbr. Chartered Life Underwriter. Membership of those who have earned the chartered life underwriter degree. Knowledge is centered on estate planning and life insurance.

co-insurance: a clause in health insurance under which the insured shares in losses to the extent of the percentages required by the insurance company at the time of the loss; the insurance company usually pays 80 percent and the policyholder 20 percent. In property insurance the insured shares in the loss only if the policyholder does not insure at least to the percentage of value required by the insurance company. Therefore, if the loss is within or above the percentage required, the insured collects in full.

collision insurance: in automobile insurance, covers the insured's own vehicle if it collides with another vehicle or object; does not cover bodily injury or property damage arising out of the collision.

Commissioners Standard Ordinary (CSO): a table of mortality approved by the National Association of Insurance Commissioners. This table is required as a minimum basis for use by all life insurance companies.

common disaster: in life insurance, the assumption of simultaneous death of the insured and beneficiary (as in a car accident) when there is no evidence of who died first.

completed operations insurance: liability insurance covering accidents after jobs have been completed. For example, a completed building may have a faulty elevator that does not cause trouble until a month after the contractor has finished the job. The insurance would cover bodily injury and/or property damage; this type of insurance would not pay for the elevator itself. Property insurance carried by the owner could cover the elevator.

composite rating: the overall lowest rate of premium which takes into account more than one coverage of a business, such as automobile, general liability, and products liability.

comprehensive: that part of automobile insurance which includes insurance against theft, vandalism, or fire. Does not include collision or upset.

compulsory: required by law, such as automobile insurance.

concurrent insurance: two or more policies held by a property owner with the same conditions and coverages that cover the same interest in the same property.

conditional receipt: a term used when giving a receipt for a premium paid for a life and health insurance policy; coverage is effective from date of application and health examination provided insurability is established at the examination.

consequential loss coverage: insurance for a business interruption caused by a primary loss. For example, John Smith owns a music school. A fire damaged all the school's instruments, and classes had to be suspended. The instruments were the primary loss; the loss of tuition and time was a secondary loss.

constructive total loss: a loss great enough to make the repair as costly as or more costly than the value of the property.

contractual or assumed liability insurance: a policy which covers a temporary user of a property for liability for which another is ordinarily responsible. Architects often require such a contract from a builder in order to transfer the liability for the construction away from themselves and to the builder.

contributory negligence also known as comparative negligence: the calculation of shared car damages and the calculated award due to each person.

conversion: the change from one policy to another.

convertible policy: a term life insurance policy that can be changed to a whole life insurance policy.

corridor deductible: a health insurance term to denote a deductible amount between the benefits paid by the basic plan and the beginning of the major medical plan. A case in point is a major medical plan that goes into effect after the first $10,000 of costs. If the basic plan picks up only $8,000 of these initial costs, $2,000 will be the corridor deductible.

coverage also known as protection: the insurance policy's promise of payment in case of loss, liability, indemnity, etc.

death waiver: a clause in an insurance policy which states that certain causes of death will not be covered. Which specific causes are applicable depends on the individual policy.

declination: the rejection of an application for insurance by an insurance company.

decreasing term insurance: life insurance of which the face value slowly decreases in scheduled steps from the time the policy becomes effective to the date the policy expires. The premiums remain constant. *See* term insurance

deductible: basic loss or expense the insurer must pay before an insurance policy pays benefits.

degree of risk: *see* law of large numbers

delay clause: a provision in life insurance whereby the insurer may delay for a period of no longer than six months the granting of any loan against the cash value of the policy, except to pay the premiums on the policy.

DIC: abbr. Difference in Conditions. A separate contract whenever property is involved that may need extremely broad coverage; coverage providing all risks of physical damage including earthquake and flood.

direct loss: damage which is a direct consequence of a particular peril. A fire in a car may cause a direct loss of the car.

direct-writing company: an insurance company that deals directly with its policyholders without intervention of independent agents or brokers.

disability: incapacity to work or function on the job or in private life. May be partial, total, temporary, or permanent.

disability waiver insurance: a rider available in life insurance providing that the insurance company will pay the premium if the policyholder is sick and disabled.

discovery period: the time allotted after the termination of an insurance policy or bond within which a loss or claim must be stated in order to be covered.

dividends: primarily in life insurance, the refund of a part of the premium after the company has set aside necessary reserves and made deductions for claims and expenses. There are many types of dividend insurance refunds, dividend deposits, accumulations, averaging, extras, options, etc.

dogs on home insurance banned lists: not all companies restrict dog breeds, but many do.

donee beneficiary: a beneficiary who has never paid a premium. For example, a wife would be a donee beneficiary when the husband pays for his own insurance policy and names his wife donee beneficiary. *See* beneficiary

double indemnity: a clause in life insurance providing the beneficiary double the face value in case the policyholder dies from accidental means.

dread disease policy: health insurance providing a maximum of medical expenses arising out of diseases named in the policy such as cancer.

earned premium: the amount that has been used up during the term of an insurance policy after the fee of an insurance policy is paid. A policy which has been paid for a year, after four months would have a four-month earned premium.

elimination period: the waiting period until benefits start in a health and disability policy.

encumbrance: *see* Index

endorsement: the form used to make a change on any insurance policy such as replacing an old car with a new car.

endowment: a type of life insurance that promises to pay the face value to the beneficiary if the policyholder dies before the policy is completely paid for. If the policyholder is still living when the insurance policy is paid up, the full face value will be paid to the policyholder.

Equifax: a credit information company used by insurers to obtain information on applicants and claimants. Reports are known as Retail Credit Reports.

errors and omissions insurance also known as malpractice insurance or professional liability: insurance against professional error or negligence which may cause loss and suffering.

estimated premium: an estimated fee for insurance used mainly in large businesses where group insurance such as health insurance is involved; since the size of the group is variable and affects premium costs, the true costs of premium will be known only at the end of the year. In casualty insurance, including among others workers' compensation, a final fee is determined via an audit by the insurance company at the end of the policy period.

examination: the auditing of an insurance company's books by the state for veracity.

exclusion: a peril of loss that is specifically excluded from coverage; flood, earthquake, war, nuclear reaction, etc.

expense ratio: the proportion of an insurance company's expenses to premiums.

experience: within a given time, the record of claims made to and paid out by an insurance company; determines premiums.

extended benefit: an additional agreement broadening an insurance contract.

extended term: a nonforfeiture value; the cash value of a whole life insurance policy to purchase term insurance for the face value of the original policy. *See* nonforfeiture value

face amount also known as face value: in life insurance, the full amount to be paid eventually upon the death of the insured.

facility of payment: a clause found in life insurance stating that under certain conditions, person(s) other than the beneficiary may receive payment.

Fair Credit Reporting Act: Public Law 91-508. If a client's request for insurance is declined because of poor credit rating, the applicant should be given the name of the reporting agency. The client may request a copy of the report and require an amendment of any errors in the report.

financed insurance: payment of life insurance premiums from money borrowed from the cash value of the policy.

financial responsibility law: a state law varying in degree from state to state which in essence requires insurance or other proof of the ability to pay for losses.

first to die life insurance: as the first person dies the policy pays out to the named survivor. This may be used by couples, a sole parent living with a child, or significant others living together.

flat: without service or interest charges. For example, there is no penalty charge if canceling an insurance before its expiration date.
www.lawinsider.com/dictionary/flat-premium

floater: a term referring to a policy covering movable property as long as it is within the territorial limits set in the contract. For example, a floater may be used to insure a valuable piece of jewelry.

fragmentation: a term used when several insurance companies share a larger risk by each taking a part of the coverage.

friendly fire: a fire in its right and proper place such as in a fireplace, barbecue, etc.

GL: abbr. general liability. Insurance maintained by businesses against bodily injury, property damage, and other operational hazards.

grace period: an extension of the due date for insurance premiums.

graded commission: an agent's fee that depends on class, type, or volume of insurance written.

grading schedule for cities and towns: a rating by the National Board of Fire Underwriters of areas such as cities and towns based on fire protection and water supply.

graduated life table: mortality possibilities calculated geographically and by formula.

gross premium: the net premium plus fees and other expenses.

grossline: the total limit on a specified risk or "class of business" such as a bowling alley, motel, or hotel that an insurance company is willing to accept.

group insurance: insurance bought by a group in order to benefit from lower premiums. The group may be under the umbrella of a place of employment, church, or other organization.

guaranteed funds: a provision of the Insurance Guarantee Act that insurance companies pool funds to pay unpaid claims or to bail out a company near bankruptcy. www.cga.ct.gov/current/pub/chap_704a.htm

guaranteed renewable: usually in health insurance, the right of the insured to continue the insurance for a substantial time by paying the premiums and not making any changes in the policy while the contract is in force. A premium rate change can be permissible.

hazard: anything that may increase the possibility of loss, harm, liability, or infraction on health such as a leaking roof, unsanitary conditions in an institution, etc.

HIAA: abbr. Health Insurance Association of America. Life and health insurers provide research and education and are active in Washington, D.C., all for the promotion of voluntary private health insurance. HII (Health Insurance Institute) is the branch of HIAA that concerns itself mostly with the outflow of information.

www.ahip.org

www.ahip.org/designations/health-insurance-associate-hia-designation

HMO: abbr. Health Maintenance Organization. Members pay a premium for which the individual or the family receives complete healthcare from internists and specialists who work within a network. As a rule members are not covered outside the network except for an emergency.

www.healthcare.gov/glossary/health-maintenance-organization-hmo

hold harmless agreement: *see* contractual liability insurance

homeowner's policy: a policy which provides protection against liability and other losses such as theft, fire, etc., to which a homeowner or renter is exposed.

hull insurance: special insurance for yachts, speedboats, houseboats, or cargo ships.

human life value: an estimate of the earning power of an individual from present age to retirement.

"if" clause: a clause terminating coverage when certain conditions are discovered, such as misrepresentation, fire hazards, etc.

IIA: abbr. Insurance Institute of America, Inc. An organization that develops recognized programs and gives national examinations and diplomas in most facets of insurance.

www.insuranceopedia.com

www.insuranceopedia.com/definition/2420/insurance-institute-of-america-iia

III: abbr. Insurance Information Institute. An organization that deals with public relations programs of various segments of property and liability insurance.

www.iii.org

IIS: abbr. International Insurance Seminars, Inc., also known as International Insurance Society. An organization of insurance people noted primarily for its annual seminars which allows academicians as well as insurance practitioners to exchange ideas.
www.internationalinsurance.org/events

increased cost of construction: a rise in replacement cost that may cause the price to be higher than the original building cost which may impact the insurance cost.

in kind: the right of the insurer to replace the loss with the equivalent material or object rather than with cash.

indemnify: to make good a loss.

indemnity: the repair, payment, or replacement of a loss.

inherent vice: a fault that leads to inevitable destruction and therefore not covered by the insurance.

insolvency clause also known as strike through: a stipulation that the reinsurer must pay his share of a loss even though the primary insurer has become insolvent. In bankruptcy cases the amount is paid directly to the insured and not the liquidator.

inspection: an examination usually by an independent company to check the facts about an applicant.

insurable risk: an applicant that meets the standards of the insurance company; the insurer is able to calculate the chance of loss.

insurance: a pooling of money to share an individual's losses, catastrophes, accidents and health problems; not for the profit of the individual policyholder. Costs are figured on the basis of statistics.

insurance carrier: the insurer.

insurance commissioner: the head of the state's insurance regulatory agency.

insurance policy: the contract between the insurer and the insured.

insurance services office: a rate-setting body for all lines of property and casualty insurance.

insuring agreement: the heart of a policy; states the period of the contract perils, and names the who, what, when and how of the insurance coverage.

joint insurance: life insurance written on two or more persons with benefits payable usually at the first death.

judgment rates also known as A rates: rates based on the underwriter's judgment rather than by loss experience. *See* experience

key person insurance: life or disability insurance bought by a company or employer to cover a person who contributes substantially to the success of the business.

lapsed policy: a policy that has expired because of nonpayment of premiums.

last clear chance: a term for the doctrine that one who had the very last chance to avoid an accident is liable.

law of large numbers also known as degree of risk, odds and probability: the examination of statistics during a given period and of a large number of people to calculate the ratio of loss, risk, and deaths.

ledger cost: the net cost of life insurance. The company subtracts the present cash value of the policy less the premiums paid and less all dividends.

level premium insurance: life insurance for which the premium remains the same throughout the contract. Since payments are usually less in the beginning and more in the later years, the "level" is usually the average.

level term insurance: a term policy, the face value of which remains the same from the effective date until the expiration date.

liability: money to be paid out; money owed; obligations, anticipated obligations and losses.

liability insurance: coverage against loss, unexpected damage or obligations, and responsibility to others. An automobile driver has an obligation of safety to other drivers and pedestrians as well as property.

liability limits: the maximum amount the insurance contract will pay in case of responsible obligation.

life insurance: risk sharing under which the insured gives contributions which the insurer reinvests to pay out to a beneficiary when the insured dies. There are various types of life insurance. *See* whole life and endowment

line sheet: a guide outlining the limits of liability to be assumed by the insurance for different classes of risks.

loading: the added costs of operating an insurance and the risk that losses will be greater than statistically expected. The opposite of "pure" insurance, which is only the estimated cost necessary for losses.

loan value: the amount of money that may be borrowed from the cash value of an insurance policy.

loss: 1) an insured's claim; the amount paid out by an insurance company to cover a claim; 2) the reduction of the value of a piece of property because of a peril making it difficult or expensive to insure.

loss of use insurance: coverage against inability to use whatever is insured (such as a store or a vehicle) because of damage or loss.

loss payable: in case of loss, payment provided to someone other than a policyholder. For example, a car bought with a loan would need a policy to protect the lending institution.

loss ratio: the proportion of losses to premiums.

loss reserve: the estimated liability for losses due but not yet paid.

losses incurred: total losses in a given period.

major medical: medical insurance with large deductibles that takes over where basic insurance leaves off. Covers "catastrophic" medical expenses in and out of the hospital.

malicious mischief: *see* V&MM

malinger: to feign disability to collect longer than necessary disability insurance.

malpractice insurance: coverage that protects professionals such as doctors and lawyers against claims of poor judgment and pays damages set by the court.

mass merchandising: the method of selling insurance to a group of people or businesses with common requirements; the group mails in the premium in one lump sum to one company and for one master contract.

master-servant rule: a legal term stating that employers are obligated to protect the public from employees' acts.

maturity: when a life insurance policy's face value becomes payable.

mental distress: a condition leading to a claim which is usually honored if the claimant was physically involved but not if the claimant was a bystander. Exceptions have been made in a few extreme cases.

merit rating: an individual's loss record upon which premiums depend; most commonly used in automobile insurance.

minimum rate: low premiums because risk factor is low.

misstatement of age: a uniform provision for individual life insurance policies as to what action is to be taken in misinformation about age.

moral hazard: a company or person insured against liability such as a law firm being sued or a person insured against accident who now may feel free to take chances that they would not take if they were not insured.

morbidity rate: statistics in given diseases, disorders, related age groups, and groups in general in comparison to well persons, all within a given time.

mortgage insurance: a policy promising to pay, in case of death, a mortgagor's mortgage completely or to continue installment payments.

motor vehicle record (MVR): a driver's record of accidents and convictions in his or her home state. The state may also ask for the driver's conviction notices in other states. Insurance companies look at the MVR to determine the underwriting of the auto insurance.

Mutual Benefit Association: an organization to which no fixed premiums are paid but members are levied costs of losses as they occur.

Mutual Insurance Company: a company of which each policyholder is a member. Dividends may or may not be paid to the policyholders.

negligence: the failure of care by action and/or omission; lack of reasonable prudence. There are in legal terminology many types of negligence: gross (willful), comparative (proportionally), contributory and presumed.

no-fault insurance: a type of automobile insurance that stipulates that no matter whose fault an automobile accident is, the victim can collect damages and medical expenses directly from his or her insurance; practiced by most states, but not by all, and there are major variations from state to state.

noncancelable: the same as guaranteed renewable, except that the premium must remain as stated in the policy at the time of issue.

nonforfeiture value: the value of a life policy when it is terminated by anything other than death. The value is expressed either in cash, extended term, or reduced paid-up insurance.

noninsurable risk: a risk possibility so high that insurance cannot be written on it; a risk possibility that cannot be measured.

nonownership automobile liability: protection against liability when someone other than the insured drives the car in question.

omnibus clause: a clause that extends coverage to include persons other than the policyholder.

other insurance clause: a statement of what is to be done in case a hazard, liability, or claim is covered by more than one policy.

overinsured: the condition in which an individual has purchased more insurance than needed to replace a loss so that it becomes profitable for the insured to have a loss and make a claim. In some states loss recovery is limited to actual loss sustained regardless of how much insurance was originally purchased.

package insurance: one policy including several coverages that would ordinarily be in separate policies.

PAR: abbr. participating. An insurance company that distributes dividends (when declared) to its policyholders.

partnership insurance: the mutual insurance of partners in a business, each partner insuring the other. If one dies, the other can then afford to buy the decedent's partnership in the business from the heirs.

Paul versus Virginia: a landmark case in 1869. The Supreme Court decided that insurance is a business and not commerce and therefore should be regulated by each state and not by the federal government.

peril: the cause of a possible loss.

permanent disability: usually defined as the inability of the insured to perform his or her usual and regular occupation.

physical hazard: *see* hazard

policy: the complete insurance contract including the name of the insurer, insured, riders, clauses and endorsements.

policy dividend: in some types of insurance, the return of part of the fee; usually the difference between gross premium charged and the actual costs as calculated according to the company's actuarial formula.

policy loan: a loan made by the insurance company to the owner of a life insurance policy using the life insurance's cash value as security.

pool: a method of reinsurance. Often a group of insurance companies will form a group and proportion the risk and premiums among themselves so that the cost of the loss is not too great for any one company. Automobile drivers with high liability records are placed in a pool insurance. Commercial aircrafts, because of their need for high coverage, are in a pool insurance.

portfolio reinsurance: the assumption of the reinsurer of all or part of the ceding insurer's business in one or all categories. *See* reinsurance and cede

portfolio return: the resumption by a ceding company of a portfolio formerly reinsured.

preferred risk: a risk deemed less risky than the average on which it was calculated.

preliminary term: insurance issued to cover risk up to a certain date at which time the policyholder may wish to renew, always paying premiums on this particular date.

premium: the fee of specified insurance protection for a specified period.

present value: the present worth of premiums which, if invested at certain interest rates, will at a future date have an increased value. The present value of the money is less than at some future date. This is used primarily in life insurance calculations where premiums may be paid on a monthly basis.

presumed negligence also known as res ipsa loquitur: a legal term meaning "the facts speak for themselves." An injury or damage occurred because of the negligence of the one responsible; for example, the owner of a house who has an exceedingly slippery waxed kitchen floor may cause someone to fall.

primary coverage: the amount covered after the deductible; coverage from the first dollar.

primary insurer: in reinsurance, the one who originated the business and ceded it.

principal sum: claim or benefits paid in one sum, especially when a contract provides benefits for accidental death or dismemberment.

prior approval rating forms: the term used to show that rate changes must be approved by the state insurance department before the company can use them.

private mortgage insurance: *see* Index

probability: the chances of an event occurring expressed in a formula between zero and ten, and calculated on a fraction basis.

producer: one who sells insurance; an agent or solicitor.

prohibited list: a list of types of risks an insurance company will not insure.

pro rata: includes more than one insurance where each insurer is proportionally accountable.

protected risk: a piece of property within the area of a fire department.

protection: coverage under the terms in an insurance policy.

public adjuster: a licensed person who represents the insured for a fee in a loss; assumes duties of the insured making an inventory of the losses, getting estimates for repairs and negotiating a settlement with the insurance company.

pure loss cost: a ratio used by insurance companies for a given period to figure out their losses of reinsurance plus allocated loss expenses compared to gross earned premiums.

pure premium: the part of the net fee needed to pay expected losses; used to determine insurance rates.

pure risk: a fifty-fifty chance as to whether there will be a loss or gain.

rate: the cost of insurance figured per unit. For example, in property insurance one insures per $100 of value. The premium is the rate times the number of units of insurance purchased. Thus if a piece of property costs $1,000, and it costs $1 per $100 of value to insure, one would multiply ten $100 units times $1. The premium would be $10.

rating bureau: a private organization which concerns itself with data on hazards, risks, rates in various geographic areas, and the compilation and measurements of such data necessary to insurance companies.
www.irmi.com/categories

rating class: the degree and category a risk is considered.

recapture: the taking back by a ceding company of the insurance it ceded. *See* cede

reciprocal insurance exchange: an incorporated group of individuals who mutually insure each other, each assuming a portion of risk.

reimbursement: the payment of a loss covered by the policy.

reinsurance: the spreading of a risk too large for one insurer by sharing the risk as well as a portion of the premium with another company.

reinsurance broker: an individual or organization who seeks out reinsurance for ceding companies. *See* cede and reinsurance

renewal certificate: an official statement used to renew a policy and uphold all the provisions in the original document; keeps the original document valid.

replacement cost: when the insurance provides complete replacement coverage without deducting depreciation.

rider: a waiver, an endorsement, a paragraph, or a clause attached to a policy. It may be to delete, expand, or add a coverage.

risk: the uncertainty of an outcome when a chance of loss exists; coverage of a person or thing.

residual value: *see* Index

safe driver plan: a form of merit rating for automobile drivers; each violation and certain traffic accidents are given points which in turn affect drivers' automobile insurance premiums.

salvage: a property taken over by an insurer to reduce loss.

second to die life insurance: a policyholder can name someone other than a spouse such as a child, grandchild, or a friend as beneficiary.

settlement: a claim payment after the insured and insurer have agreed on the amount.

shock loss: a loss so great that it affects the insurer's rates.

short rate premium: a premium for less than a year (most premiums are for one year). If the insured cancels after six months, his rate will be higher than 50 percent of one year.

standard policy: identical insurance regardless of which insurance company issues the policy; insurance in compliance with state law; insurance issued to a standard risk. *See* standard risk

standard risk: a person entitled to insurance without extra rating or special restrictions. A term especially used in health and life insurance.

state fund: those funds set up by the state government to finance mandatory insurance. Varies from state to state in that it may be monopolistic or competitive.

statutory reserve: as required by law, the reserve needed by every insurer.

stop loss: 1) a provision to limit losses to protect the insurer from suffering too great a loss; 2) a reinsurance term whereby the reinsurer takes over only after the ceding company has incurred losses which exceed a specified loss ratio. *See* cede

subrogation clause: the right of the insurer to pursue any course of action in the company's or the insured's name against a third party who is liable for a claim which has been paid by the policyholder's company.

sub-standard: anyone posing a higher risk of filing a claim. That may include a poor driver, poor health, and other risks such as unsafe hobbies and/or jobs.

surrender: a term used in life insurance when the insured terminates his or her life insurance and is given the cash value of the policy.

term: the period of time for which a policy is issued.

term insurance: an agreement between the insured and an insurance company whereby the insurance company promises to pay the face amount of the policy if the insured dies within a specified time period. If the insured survives the period, the contract expires without value. There are many varieties of term insurance. *See* convertible policy

Many young people like term insurance because it is less expensive than other types of life insurance. Jane and Tom, for example, got married when they were both twenty years old. When they were expecting their first child they decided, even though Tom was in excellent health, that it would be wise to have a five-year term insurance policy, because they did not have any assets or savings. If something happened to Tom, Jane and the baby would have some instant assets.

time limit: the allotted period within which notice of claim and proof of loss must be submitted to an insurance company.

title insurance: *see* Index

tort insurance: liability insurance against a wrong committed against an individual. The wrong may be independent of a contract and may be considered a private wrong.

traumatic injury: physical damage to one's body caused accidentally and not from disease or illness.

tsunami damage: special insurance for buildings in a flood area or in a tidal-wave zone in order for them to be eligible for a mortgage.

underwriter: 1) the one who signs his name on the insurance contract; an insurance company itself may be the underwriter; 2) the expert who selects the risks the insurance company can accept and up to what amount and on what terms the risks can be accepted.

unearned premium: on an insurance balance sheet, those fees paid in but not yet used up on the calendar of time. For example, for car insurance paid in advance every six months, there would be five months of unearned premium after the first month has passed.

unemployment insurance: insurance against loss of income due to unemployment. Unemployment insurance is funded by payroll taxes and subject to control by both federal and state governments.

unilateral contract: an agreement in which only one party makes promises. Most insurance policies are unilateral because the insurer makes all the promises while the insured keeps the policy in force by paying the premiums.

uninsured motorists coverage: a clause found in most automobile insurance. The insurance company will pay damages for bodily injuries when their client is hit by a hit-and-run driver or by an uninsured driver. A minority of states have property damage coverage automatically included.

valuation: the appraisal of items to be insured such as jewelry, silverware, fur coats, etc.

valued policy: the statement by the policy that a determined amount will be paid in the event of a total loss.

V&MM: abbr. Vandalism and Malicious Mischief. Willful damage and destruction to property excluding theft.

vesting rights: upon termination of employment, the right to the employee's share of the money in a pension plan funded by the employer.

voidable: renderable of no legal effect by either party to a contract. The insured may void a policy by not paying his premiums, and the insurer may cancel if the insured commits certain acts.

waiver: a clause excluding liability; a clause excluding a known right; for example, the insurance company may give up its rights to collect premiums during a period of disability of the insured.

whole life insurance: insurance the face value of which is only paid upon the death of the insured; has cash value and in some cases may pay dividends.

workers' compensation: a law requiring that the employer provide insurance that will pay benefits to an employee or his or her beneficiary if the employee is injured or suffers death or disability as a result of occupational hazard.

FINANCIAL STATEMENTS

accelerated depreciation: a formula which allocates the cost of an asset over its useful life so that more of the cost is deducted from income as an expense in earlier years than in later years.

accounting: recording and summarizing an individual's or business' financial position and activities, mainly expenses and income.

accounts payable: to whom and how much a business, individual, company or corporation owes money; it may be for raw material, services and other needs. In a general ledger, accounts payable are recorded as one total sum (after individual postings).

accounts receivable: money owed to a company or an individual for products or services. Accounts receivable are listed as an asset on the balance sheet.

accumulated depreciation: the total amount of depreciation value of an asset which has been recorded since it was acquired, up to the present time period.

additional paid-in capital: additional monies or properties received from sale of capital stock above par value.

adjusted trial balance: the original balance updated by new entries. Trial balance helps a company note if its accounting debits are not greater than its credits.

administrative expenses: general expenses of a business such as rent and electricity as contrasted to expenses incurred by specific functions of the enterprise, such as selling expenses and financing costs.

allowance method: monetary need as estimated from past experiences. For example, if every year a certain percentage of customers don't pay their bills, an allowance can be calculated and deducted from accounts receivable.

amortization: the cost of an intangible asset (such as a patent, goodwill, or trademark) spread out over the life of the asset; as the expense is shown on an income statement, the value of the asset decreases. (Not to be confused with the amortization of a bond or mortgage.)

annual report: the formal statement issued yearly by a company for its stockholders, among others, showing assets, liabilities, earnings and other information of interest.

assets: anything owned by an individual or a business; includes cash, investments, receivables, and inventories as well as fixed and intangible assets such as trucks, cars and buildings.

audit: the examination of accounting records by an independent accounting firm to determine whether the financial statements are prepared in conformity with generally accepted accounting principles.

balance sheet: a summary of the assets, liabilities, and capital of a person or enterprise.

bank reconciliation: a means of explaining the difference between the bank balance on the bank statement versus the balance of cash in the ledger. For example, the difference may be due to an uncleared check, bank fees, or interest received.

book value: the sum of the assets less the sum of the liabilities of a company. Sometimes a company is worth more than the book value shows because such items as building, equipment, etc., are always presented at their depreciated values. Furthermore, a company's general reputation, trademark and track record, which are all intangibles and which contribute to a company's value, are usually unrecorded.

book value per share: the sum of the assets less the sum of the liabilities and preferred stockholders' equity of a company, divided by the number of common shares outstanding.

business segment reporting: a requirement of those companies involved in two or more lines of business to report sales and contributions to earnings by their business segments or product lines. For example, XYZ Company manufactures ten different items. Only two items sell well. It is of interest to stockholders to have a detailed report of each one of the ten lines. Otherwise, the stockholders won't know which line contributed the most to the company's profitability and if management is paying too much attention to one particular segment.

capital: funds invested in the business by stockholders; includes stocks, reinvested earnings, and preferred stock.

capital expenditure: a major addition to a business, such as buildings, equipment, tools, or vehicles.

capital structure: how money is funded in a business paralleled with all forms of debt and equity.

capitalization ratio: the ratio of debt to a company's equity. Debt includes bond issues or other types of loans, and equity includes retained earnings, preferred stock, common stock and short-term debt.

cash disbursement journal: a record of the outflow of money in cash or bank checks that shows in which account the payment ultimately was posted.

cash flow: business cash receipts (inflows) and cash disbursements (outflows). Receipts come from sales, interest, income/profit earned, and funds from the issuance of debt or stock.

Disbursements are made for supplies, rent, purchases of fixed or tangible assets, and redemption of debt or stock.

cash receipts journal: an accounting journal recording incoming money.

changes in components of working capital: a statement presented by a corporation showing the effect of its financing and investing activities in its current assets and liabilities. It includes increases and decreases in current assets such as cash, marketable securities, accounts receivable, and inventories. Also shown are increases and decreases in current liabilities such as accounts payable, accrued liabilities, current maturity of long-term debt, dividends payable, and income and taxes.

chart of accounts: the categories a business uses to record transactions which affect its daily finances. It may use numerical codes as well as the title of each account.

classified balance sheet: a highly detailed statement breaking down assets and liabilities to specific headings such as current and long-term. For example, assets may have headings for intangible assets, fixed assets, inventory, accounts receivable, and cash.

combined or overall coverage: *see* times interest earned

consolidated balance sheet: a balance sheet showing the financial condition of a corporation and its subsidiaries.

contingent liabilities: liabilities whose payment depends on the outcome of a future event; may include goods sold under warranty, court outcome of product defects or new tax assessment.

controlling account: an account in the general ledger which has a subsidiary ledger which lists more details than numbers such as debit and credit of other accounts as well as individual transactions.

cost of goods sold: the total expenses of inventory at the time of sale. For a retail business it is the cost of inventory purchased, sales help, rent/maintenance of store, etc., while for manufacturing business it is the cost of raw material, maintenance of location, labor and other overhead.

CPA (Certified Public Accountant): an accountant who has passed all parts of a state exam qualifying him or her for a license to practice accounting.

current assets: those assets a company expects to receive, turn into cash or use up within a year or less; included may be cash, accounts receivable, inventories, prepaid rent and supplies.

current liability: the money presently owed and due by a company within the next twelve months or less.

current maturity of long-term debt: the amount due in the next year; some debts may require partial annual repayment over a period of years.

current ratio also known as working capital ratio: a figure used by financial analysts to measure sufficient levels of working capital by dividing the amount of assets by the amount of liabilities. A higher ratio is better.

debt to asset: used by companies to calculate their total debt in proportion to their assets. The formula used is to divide total debt or liabilities by total assets. The lower the number is, the healthier the company's equity.

deferral: for business purposes, postponement of the recognition of a sale or an expense until the money is used up, or postponement of the recognition of an expense until the merchandise is used up. For example, a monthly magazine may receive money for a one year subscription, but may post the income as unearned revenue until it delivers the twelve issues.

deficit: the condition of a company whose retained earnings show a debit balance due to operational losses.

depletion accounting: an accounting practice in bookkeeping where charges are made against earnings made from the use of natural resources. The accounting allows for the fact that the natural resource in question may eventually be used up. These resources include oil, gas, timber, coal, and metals.

depreciation: the recording of the yearly depreciation of a fixed asset as an expense such as machines, computers, and buildings.

dividend payout: the percentage of earnings on the common stock that is paid out in dividends. Some companies keep a part of the earnings in order to expand the company or to have an extra cash flow.

dividend return: the yearly income one receives from a stock. John Smith owns 100 shares of XYZ stock which he bought at $25 a share for a total value of $2,500. His dividend is $200 a year: 8 percent of his total investment or $2 per share.

dividends payable: preferred or common stock dividends or both declared by the board of directors but not yet paid. Because they have been declared, it is a legal obligation and a liability of a company.

double-entry bookkeeping: a system of accounting in which each entry is recorded twice, once on the debit side and once on the credit side. For example, an individual received $10,000 for a job done. It is recorded on the credit side. The receiver of the money knows that the money will be used for rent, for paying insurance and a recent credit card bill and thus places all these amounts on the debit side. There is $2,000 left which will be placed in a pension account and recorded on the debit side since it will no longer be part of the $10,000 originally received.

earnings before income tax: operating profit minus interest owed to stockholders and other debt holders.

ending inventory: the value of the amount of material or goods available at the end of a fiscal period.

equity: the claims of the stockholders against the assets of the company.

expenses: in bookkeeping terminology, any costs involving the running of the company. Expenses may be broken down into categories and units such as sales, production, research, and administration, as well as general reduction of the value of assets.

FIFO (first-in, first-out): a system of recording ending inventory in which the earliest items purchased for the inventory are figured as sold first.

financial reporting: a business' entire operations including its divisions, additional companies owned, product lines, and real property, giving financial information in greater specifics than an annual report.

fiscal year: a regular period of time in which a company does its accounting before starting a new twelve-month accounting period. Not all companies are able to use the calendar year. For example, department stores which do most of their business at Christmastime find it difficult to end their year on December 31.

fixed assets: assets with a life in excess of one year; may include buildings, land, machinery, equipment, and motor vehicles.

fixed charges also known as fixed expenses: costs that do not vary with volume of activity.

freight in: an account entry showing transportation expenses of inventory.

funds: net working capital available.

general journal: all details of a business' account recording including the date of any transaction, the amount involved and if it is an asset, revenue, liability, expense, equity or any other specifics. This information may later be used in the appropriate ledgers.

general ledger: the principal ledger containing income and debit statements providing the needed balance sheets.

going concern: a business doing so well according to the accounting ledgers that it will not go out of business within the foreseeable future.

gross profit: direct profit. Only the direct cost of the goods (such as raw material and labor) is subtracted from the sale of the goods. Such costs as advertising are not included.

gross sales: the measure of goods sold before deductions, returns, price allowances and discounts.

horizontal analysis: a method of comparing statements by showing the rate and amount of change across columns of statements from period to period.

index: a means of measuring against and comparing to a base year (sample year) by percentages.

intangible assets: assets that do not have a physical presence but contribute to the company's future and growth. Goodwill, franchises, trademarks, patents and copyrights are all intangible assets.

interest coverage ratio: *see* times interest

interest expenses: interest paid or due on debts and listed as liabilities to a company.

inventory: raw materials, work in process as well as finished products measured at cost or market value and listed as an asset on the balance sheet.

inventory turnover ratio: a figure calculated by dividing the cost of goods sold in the most recent year by the average of the inventory of the last twelve months. For example, Jan's dress shop sold $12,000 worth of blouses within the past year; the average number of blouses in the inventory within the last twelve months was 600; the turnover ratio of a blouse was $^{\$12,000}/_{600}$ or a cost of 5 to 1.

liabilities: all claims against a business or person such as unpaid bills, taxes, rent, wages, loans, debts, promissory notes, and interest dues.

LIFO (last-in, first-out): an inventory costing or valuation method which assumes that inventory bought most recently is sold first. It typically is used by a business in which a product is constantly improved such as a tech company. *See* FIFO

liquidity ratio: a measure of how quickly a company can raise or provide cash. The ratio is derived by subtracting inventories from current assets and dividing by the current liabilities:

$$\frac{\text{CURRENT ASSETS} - \text{INVENTORIES}}{\text{CURRENT LIABILITIES}}$$

long-term liabilities also known as long-term debts or fixed liabilities: in a business, any services, obligations, mortgages, bonds and other debts that are not due for a year or more.

marketable securities: securities carried in the balance sheet and computed at cost or fair value.

minimum legal capital: *see* Index

net asset value per share: *see* Index

net income for the year: a term for earnings or profits after all costs have been deducted. More commonly called "the bottom line."

net loss: the amount arrived at when expenses are greater than profit.

net pay: wages minus all deductions such as social security, taxes, benefits, etc.

net sales: total cash earned in a business minus discounts, sales returns and other allowances.

operating profit: a figure arrived at by deducting costs of goods, selling and administrative expenses and depreciation from sales; taxes and interest charges are not deducted.

operating profit margin: profit calculated as a percentage of sales before deducting depreciation, interest and taxes; this margin is considered a basic indicator of efficiency of operations.

operations: the breakdown of day-to-day sales, earnings, costs, and expenses, omitting non-regular expenses such as buying a new fleet of trucks.

paid-in capital: the amount originally invested in the business by the stockholders at par value of the shares. Paid-in capital is listed on the balance sheet as a segment of stockholders' equity.

par: abbr. Performance Audit Report. The dollar amount of a company's common shares on the balance sheet.

posting: the placement of a transaction into a ledger from a journal. Both the ledger and journal show the page number from which the information came or to which it was transferred.

purchase discount account: an account showing a credit or savings because a bill or bills were paid within a given early period.

quarterly data: a presentation of financial results of a business on a three-month basis.

receivables: bills owed to the company and placed in the assets column of the ledger.

residual value also known as salvage value: the resale or scrap value of a piece of equipment when it has reached the end of its usefulness to the company. This estimation is subtracted from the cost of the equipment to arrive at the amount of depreciation.

retained earnings: accumulated earnings reinvested in the business. Essentially, it is a summation of annual earnings minus dividends and other charges.

sales-to-fixed-asset ratio: a financial relationship determined by dividing annual sales by the value of property, plant and equipment. The ratio shows if funds are productively invested.

statement of income: a statement showing sales less cost, expenses, taxes, interest and depreciation.

straight-line method of depreciation: a formula used to calculate the total amount of depreciation allowed to a company's assets (e.g., machines, vehicles, plant) over their estimated life. One takes the original cost of the equipment minus salvage value and divides by the number of years to be depreciated. For example, if Company X buys a car for $8,000 to be used for four years and which, after four years, can still be sold for $4,000, the annual depreciation according to this formula is $1,000.

voucher system: an internal control system used in large companies by which any expense or purchase is recorded for each check drawn.

worksheet: a rough draft in which an accountant summarizes the data needed to complete a final statement.

INVESTING IN A SMALL BUSINESS

ACE (Active Corps of Executives): *see* SCORE

advertisement: the means by which the public is made aware of a product; includes 1) the choice of medium (internet's social media, cellphone, newspaper, television, radio, magazine, billboard, or direct mail), 2) the cost effective rate (amount of business to be generated from the investment), and 3) figuring out the required investment level; the amount in dollars required to produce an effective business campaign in the chosen medium.

advice: an acknowledgment in a form letter to a customer from a bank indicating that it has executed the instructions of its customer such as to make a transfer or a payment or to credit or receive money, checks, drafts, securities, or other documents. A bank also receives incoming or returning advices from correspondent banks.

www.helpwithmybank.gov/glossary/index-glossary.html

angel investor: a private investor or often a well-situated family member who provides funds for a start-up idea usually in exchange for equity in the company. The financial aid may be a one-time sum or yearly seed money for the start-up period.

authority: the ultimate responsibility borne by the owner(s) in all decision-making.

average: a number typical of a group of numbers, such as the average wage, or average sale.

average markup: the practice of using the same percentage markup for each item when a business carries many items.

balance of trade: the national difference in money value of national imports and exports.

banker's acceptance: a trade draft guaranteed by an accepting bank; the accepting bank is the one that guarantees payment for the goods.

bankruptcy: a declaration of insolvency, after which financial affairs are administered by the court through a receiver or trustee; may be 1) voluntary: applied for and granted by the court, or 2) involuntary: petitioned for by creditors and granted by the court.

brand: a name, term, symbol, sign, and/or design used to identify the product of a firm.

break-even volume: the basic amount of sales needed to pay for keeping a business running without loss or profit. Total fixed costs divided by selling price minus variable cost per unit equals the basic break-even point.

broker also known as merchandise agent: an agent without title to merchandise what he or she sells, who receives income from commissions and fees.

Bureau of the Census: an agency that reports vital and valuable statistics on demographics throughout the nation with some studies of special interest to businesses.

business liquidation auction: a sale at which equipment from heavy machinery to office equipment—all valuable assets—is auctioned to the highest bidder.

charting revenues: keeping track of income from units sold. If a manufacturer has to sell 300 units in order to cover all his costs, it is important for the company to keep track of its income.

collection agency: a firm engaged in collecting overdue accounts for others.

Commerce Business Daily: the United States Department of Commerce's information publication issued by the United States Government Publishing Office to provide notices of proposed government procurement actions, contract awards, sales of government property, and other procurement information. Each edition contains approximately 500–1,000 notices. Each notice appears in the CBD only once.

All federal procurement offices are required to announce proposed procurement actions over $25,000 and contract awards over $25,000 that are likely to result in the award of any subcontracts in the CBD.

www.commerce.gov

www.govinfo.gov/help/cbd

conglomerate: *see* Index

consignment sales: products not paid for at the time of delivery to sales outlet; products to be paid for only when sold.

Consumer Price Index: the rise or fall of the cost of goods to the consumer as compared to a base year; a means of tracking inflation.

controlling: comparing actual results to planned results and taking corrective action; sufficient ownership of shares in a corporation or membership in an LLC to be able to control key decisions and directions in a corporation. *See* LLC

cooperative: a group of small companies with similar products, services, or interests, banded together for economic advantages. The cooperators are shareholders in the cooperative. The most common are agricultural markets, real estate groups, and consumer cooperatives.

corporation: a separate legal entity entirely apart from its owner(s); may have sole ownership or may have stockholders.

A corporation continues to function regardless of the death or departure of its stockholders; in most cases, creditors have claims only against the assets of the corporation. *See* legal personality

correlation: the relationship between two or more variables.

delinquent accounts: accounts receivable overdue.

demography: the study of population, including density, growth rates, occupational trends, income levels, birth and death rate and consumer behavior.

Department of Commerce: a branch of the federal government; assists in international and national trade, gives grants to help build public facilities essential to industrial and commercial development, and makes available world and national trade data and educational materials; responsible for a wide range of regulation enforcement.

Department of Labor: the federal department concerned with labor-management affairs, regulations, mediation, and labor law enforcement as well as education.

director: a manager of a corporation, bank or other business institution. Federal and state laws prescribe as to who may and may not be elected director to certain types of business institutions. *See* directors in "Stock Market Trading Terms"

discount: a reduction in price. There are various types of discounts:

> 1) *trade discounts:* the reduced price offered by the manufacturer or wholesaler to the retailer.
>
> 2) *quantity discounts:* the reduction of price in relation to the size of the purchase.
>
> 3) *cumulative quantity discounts:* the totaling of consecutive orders to qualify for a discount.
>
> 4) *cash discount:* the percentage amount permitted off a bill when paid within ten days.

5) *seasonal discounts:* the reduced price of seasonal items such as skis or air conditioners when bought off-season.

6) *employee incentive plan:* awards in the form of either extra pay or pay by the amount produced rather than by the hour, or prizes such as paid vacation for better-than-average production.

entrepreneur: someone with capital or who knows how to raise capital who conceives and develops business(es); someone who takes risks and responsibility, and expects to take profits from the business he or she conceives.

exchange control: the act of limiting or banning the flow of local currency into dollars.

Federal Trade Commission: an independent federal agency acting as a trade regulatory body; responsible for laws assuring free and fair competition, interpreting antitrust laws, and laws protecting the consumer against deceptive practices. www.ftc.gov

fictitious name statement: a legal record of who actually owns a business if a business is run under a fictitious name. In the case of a corporation, a fictitious name is any name other than the stated name in the articles of incorporation.

financial analyst: an expert who interprets data, statistics, yields, costs and future trends in order to increase business.

FOB: abbr. free on board. Items to be delivered to the specified destination are transported free up to the time they are placed on a public carrier. It is the point where the seller relinquishes ownership and the buyer accepts ownership of the products purchased in a specific transaction.

foreign correspondent: a bank in a foreign country acting for, and maintaining money for, a domestic bank.

foreign exchange rate: the number of foreign currency exchange units for each dollar.

franchise: a company that may represent and sell a product or services of a parent company in a specific territory; may also be a distribution or producing concern. Depending on the contract, the parent company profits by either outright payment, a share of the receipts, and/or agreement by the franchise to buy supplies or equipment from the parent organization.

fringe benefits: financial advantages and supplementary rewards other than salaries such as insurance and pension plans.

general partner(s): the same as a proprietor, except that more than one person is pooling efforts. A contract declares rights and responsibility in the operation of the firm.

graph: a chart, diagram, or picture showing the relationships of data to each other.

gross national product (GNP): a national market value comprised of national income (total earnings of labor and property) plus product accounts (national production of all goods and services produced in a year); a national total of consumer purchases, government purchases, gross private domestic investments, and export of goods and services; helps to chart the national economic trend including prosperity, recession, and depression, and to estimate changes in the standard of living of the population.

holding company: a business which owns the securities of another—in most cases with voting rights.

image: the company as visualized by the target population; a message that management creates and may change at any time. For example, packaging helps to create a view of the company.

independent contractor: an individual who signs a form agreeing to perform certain duties on a contractual basis rather than as an employee.

index: *see* Index

index number: in business, a percentage used to compare calculations and figures as costs or prices within a standard period.

industrial designer: an artist who takes an invention and houses it attractively; used by automobile manufacturers, washing-machine manufacturers, etc.

institutional advertising: advertising aimed at creating goodwill for a company. An example is an oil company's advertisement explaining how they protect wildlife while drilling for oil.

inventory: all the items, goods, merchandise and materials held by a business for selling in the market to earn a profit. *See* LIFO and FIFO

key person insurance: *see* Index.

labor laws: federal and state legislation pertaining to employees; regulations concerning wages, hours, working conditions, disability, unemployment compensation, and social security contributions.
www.dol.gov

law of diminishing returns: a term describing the concept that the rate of yield beyond a certain point does not increase in proportion to additional investments.

legal personality: an organization such as a government or business which can sue or be sued, buy and sell property, and in general assume obligations and liabilities.

letter of credit: *see* Index

licenses: state or professional permits to practice a profession or open a business; a means of regulating business, protecting public health, safety, zoning, and in some cases, public morality.

LLC: abbr. limited liability corporation. Formed by two or more individuals in which at least one partner is fully liable for all the debts of the business, but other partners known as the limited partners have a liability only to the extent of their investment. Mary Smith wanted to open a restaurant but she did not have enough capital. She offered a limited partnership to her brother and two friends of 10 percent of the total value of the business for each limited partner at a cost of $10,000 each. Mary would run the restaurant and make all the decisions. Each partner would receive 10 percent of the restaurant's profit as long as he kept his money invested in the business. If Mary went broke, each partner would be liable for not more than his investment. Each partner could also sell his partnership to a fellow partner or to an outsider depending on how the partnership agreement was drawn up.

loss leaders: in retailing, special inexpensively-priced merchandise offered to complement higher-priced lines and to build store traffic.

management consultant: an independent contractor who advises management on the most effective way of achieving its goal.

management controls: a term used to denote the capacity to be in touch with each unit in a business and to be able to respond to changes, adjustments, and needs.

managerial skills: the capacity to cope with responsibility and guide others to carry out the work; may include technical skills, human skills, and conceptual skills.

market research: a survey to project an estimated demand for a product, evaluate type and quality of competition and how affordable the product is to the general populace on a national, state, and local basis; the research should indicate the product's success probability.

markup: the difference between cost of an item and its selling price.

markup percentage: the markup price expressed in percentages; calculations include cost of the item, the cost of selling the item, and allowance for desired profit.

mean: the sum of a group of numbers divided by the number of individual numbers used.

median: the midpoint of numbers arranged from lowest to highest.

merchandising: those business functions dealing with presenting and selling goods and ideas; includes advertising, display, promotion and direct selling.

merger: *see* Index

micro lender: the definition of a lender who will give a loan to an individual or a small business who lacks access to conventional banking. There are usually higher fees for a micro lender's financial services.

mode: the number that occurs most frequently in a series of data.

motivation: the reason a worker wants to carry out his or her job.

national brands: brands owned by national manufacturers. *See* brand

National Small Business Association: describes itself as a "nonpartisan organization, with decades of small business advocacy expertise from our long-serving leadership, to our knowledgeable and well-connected government affairs team—we are proud to be the nation's first small-business advocacy organization"; known for being concerned with education, foreign trade, labor and taxes.
www.nsba.biz/about

Occupational Safety and Health Act (OSHA): a federal law with approximately 22,000 regulations designed to protect employees from work-related accidents, poor illumination, unmarked fire exits, inadequate washrooms and other hazards and sanitation infractions; businesses are required to display at the place of work occupational OSHA posters. OSHA also provides training, education, outreach and needed assistance.

www.osha.gov/aboutosha

oligopoly: the domination of an industry by a few large companies.

operating budget: current income and expenditures; does not include capital items.

operating level: the amount of inventory required to maintain normal operations.

organizational chart: the chain of command and reporting structure in a company.

packaging: 1) merchandise—such as soap powder, perishible foods, etc.—that because of its nature needs to be put in a carton or other container; 2) the means used to present a product in the most attractive, salable way.

parity business: a business in which products and services are very much alike.

patent: the right of exclusive proprietorship of an invention granted by the government for a specific period of time.

patent office: part of the US Department of Commerce that administers federal trademark laws and all matters pertaining to the granting of patents.

www.uspto.gov

penetration pricing: the practice of selling a new product at a low price to induce a large volume of sales; the profit comes from the volume, and the low price discourages fellow manufacturers who have not yet produced the product to compete.

personnel turnover: a term used in personnel referring to how often employees in a company have to be replaced because they are unhappy or because the employees were poorly chosen to begin with.

positioning: stressing unique selling points, emphasizing specific market segments, and setting targets; appealing to an identifiable market such as teenagers or senior citizens.

price leader: the item which sets the price and competitors follow suit.

price-lining: offering merchandise at a limited number of set prices in order to simplify the selling job and make the choice easier for the consumer. For example, a store may offer two prices for hosiery, a 99¢ line and a $1.99 line.

pricing: establishing a price for goods or services. There are two methods: below the market, and above the market. A general rule is that a small sales volume requires a relatively high markup, and a large sales volume can bear a reduced markup.

primary-demand advertising: an attempt to increase demand for a type of product—such as cheese, all-cotton clothes, etc.—rather than for a brand; usually sponsored by trade associations.

private brands: brands owned by middlemen such as retailers. *See* brand

Producer Price Index: a guideline reflecting the rise or fall of prices for finished goods; includes costs of raw material and general manufacturing costs.

production planning: preparation for the best use of machines, raw materials, and employees.

promoter: 1) one who shows a business, usually a new one, to advantage; 2) a group or organization that plans, creates, and organizes ideas, companies and corporations.

proprietor: 1) a person who forms and operates a business; the simplest form of ownership in which business income is taxed as personal income and the owner is personally liable for all claims against the business; 2) a legal title to anything such as an automobile, home, or a patent or design.

psychological pricing: a method of pricing based on a common belief that an uneven price such as $3.98 appears less expensive to the customer than a rounded number such as $4.00; some retailers choose an uneven number because it forces the clerk to give change and lessens the possibility of a clerk pocketing the even amount of dollars.

public relations: the effort toward developing a favorable public image of a business by projecting positive publicity or doing good works such as donating free merchandise to a fundraiser or making known the company's good works; for example, "we work to keep our community clean."

purchasing: the process of obtaining material for a company.

qualified products list: prepared by various government agencies for their purchasing requirements; a list containing the products and manufacturers that have met essential government specifications. *See* Commerce Business Daily
www.governmentbids.com/cgi/en/bidding.advice.articles/ Article/business-opp-with-the-federal-government

quota: a limit on the amount of a particular item that can legally be imported.

SCORE (Service Corps of Retired Executives) supplemented by ACE (Active Corps of Executives): both provide experienced men and women who volunteer their time to assist free of charge those who want their business problems analyzed and dealt with, and who in general need an experienced daily hand. SCORE has chapters around the country which are partners with the US Small Business Administration. A not-for-profit organization (501c3), it provides free mentoring and low-cost seminars for entrepreneurs and small business owners. www.score.org

primary data and secondary data: primary data has to be researched and tabulated; secondary data is economical and conveniently on hand.

silent partner: a general partner who is inactive and anonymous except to the active partner(s); depending on the contract, carries unlimited liabilities for the obligations of the business.

skimming: a method of pricing whereby a manufacturer charges a higher price for a new product because it is novel, and later, when competition enters the market, reduces the price.

Small Business Administration: an agency created by the federal government to offer financial assistance, procurement assistance, and advocacy of small business and management assistance; has more than 100 offices throughout the nation with special programs to help minorities, veterans, and the socially and economically disadvantaged; has valuable information on small business' insurance needs, risks, taxes, etc.
www.sba.gov

Small Business Institute: those universities and colleges that enter into formal contracts with the supervised management counseling to participating small businesses.
smallbusinessinstitute.wildapricot.org

standardization: a term to describe the manufacture of identical or uniform goods.

survey: questions asked by phone, mail, social media, or in public to find out product preferences, needs and whatever else will help a business.

syndicate: a group of individuals and/or investment firms, banks and stockbrokers who are temporarily associated together under one manager for some specific business venture; for example, to underwrite a particular security or to invest in a large real estate undertaking such as a shopping center or office complex.

systems analyst: an expert who interprets the company's needs for information and devises a computer program that will process the data.

table: a means of presenting data.

tariff: a tax on imported goods.

trademark: a brand given legal protection so that the owner has exclusive rights to its use. *See* brand

traffic flow: data on foot and vehicular traffic that can advance or impede a business. For instance, a retail store will want to be where there is much foot traffic; a manufacturing concern will want to be near public transportation so that its workers can get to work.

trust: any business or company owning a combination of businesses for the purpose of greater profit or eliminating competition. Antitrust laws restrict the operations of business trusts.

truth in advertising: a provision of laws that control advertising and prohibit misleading statements; most of the laws are in the hands of the Federal Trade Commission. www.ftc.gov/news-events/topics/truth-advertising

uniform delivery pricing: the same delivery price regardless of transportation costs and distance. *See* zone pricing

variables: a term used by statisticians to denote changeable factors.

venture capital: the name for the money private investors put up for start-up or already newly formed companies they feel will succeed. It may also include advice and expertise from the investors and often equities in the company.

withholding tax: social security and other federal and state taxes the employer must withhold from the employee's

wages. The Internal Revenue Service and state tax agencies can supply all the information needed.
www.irs.gov/payments/tax-withholding

zone pricing: an arrangement by which customers pay for delivery according to the distance from the manufacturer to the point of delivery. *See* uniform delivery pricing

CRYPTOCURRENCY

Since cryptocurrency is completely managed on the internet, the words used in the cryptocurrency system are a novel set of tech words defining how exactly the currency is dealt with on the internet. As you read the various cryptocurrency definitions you might come across a word within the definition itself that is foreign to you. Don't despair. Chances are, that very word is separately listed and defined in this chapter. It is also important to note that as this book goes into print the United States government does not back any cryptocurrency. The United States dollar is backed by the power of the nation's basic existence including its democracy, justice system and military protection.

address: no cryptocurrency coin can be held without an address. Since all transactions are done online, the address is a long chain of letters, numbers and symbols to make it unique.

algorithmic trading: the original definition of algorithm is a step-by-step method of solving a mathematical problem. Algorithmic trading done online in the cryptocurrency world is a methodology for transacting orders applying automated and pre-programmed trading instructions to account for variables such as price, timing and volume.

altcoin: any crypto coin that is not a bitcoin. It is a cryptocurrency that works in a similar fashion to Bitcoin but with refinements such as being able to process transactions faster.

bitcoin also known as BTC: the first cryptocurrency, first founded in 2008.

blockchain: a public ledger of transactions online that keeps owners' information anonymously.

candlestick chart: an easy to understand graph depicting the highs and lows for a given time of a centralized cryptocurrency exchange. High is delineated in green and low in red.

CBDC: abbr. Central Bank Digital Currency. As this book goes into print the only central bank money available to the general public in the United States are Federal Reserve notes (i.e., physical currency). Cryptocurrency is not guaranteed by the United States Federal Reserve.

centralized: controlled by a single entity or managed in one location.

code: a set-up of symbols—be it letters, numbers, various colors, or musical notes—to convey a message. The Morse Code is known as such, and today cryptocurrency has its own codes to transmit and store data.

coin: currency with a numerical value such as a bitcoin, ether, or tether, each registered on its individual blockchain.

coinbase: the centralized cryptocurrency exchange publicly traded on NASDAQ.

cold storage: any crypto assets which may include the wallet kept off the network on a specialized USB or other offline devices preventing hackers on the internet from procuring it. *See* hot wallet and wallet

crypto: the syllable crypto is defined in dictionaries as secret or hidden; not publicly admitted.

crypto assets: an account of an individual's ownership of cryptocurrency as well as non-fungible tokens (for example, artwork or a gem), recorded in a distributed ledger such as a blockchain. *See* NFT

crypto coin: a digital currency which can be used to make payments.

cryptocurrency: a digital currency accounted for in a decentralized manner using cryptographic computer codes. There are over 19,000 different cryptocurrencies. Bitcoin was the first cryptocurrency.

crypto discord server: an online social platform catering to those interested in crypto events, crypto market, retail funds, trading, coin projects, and all other information having to do with cryptocurrency.

cryptocurrency exchange: a computerized marketplace where cryptocurrency can be bought and sold. A trusted third person or party, much as we would trust a bank, may be used to execute transactions. Commissions or transaction fees are charged for the service. *See* decentralized

cryptography: the methods of secret code writing which may already exist or may be newly organized.

CTP also known as cryptoexchanges: abbr. Cryptoasset Trading Platforms. An online method where buyers and sellers of crypto assets can do trades and transactions.

DAO: abbr. Decentralized Autonomous Organization. As the name implies, the organization functions by computer code which is governed by anonymous users who vote on recommendations with crypto tokens. We are used to a company's management taking care of such orders. DAO completely replaces management with software technology.

dApps: applications used on the blockchain to install a smart contract. *See* smart contract and Ethereum

decentralized: controlled by several rather than one single entity or location.

DEFI: abbr. Decentralized Finance. Whereby finances are carried out without the involvement of a middle authority such as a financial institution or a governmental department, like the SEC. *See* SEC

digital: paperless, computerized.

digital asset: any asset that exists only digitally.

Ethereum: like Bitcoin, has its own currency with its own value. Ethereum allows users to create their own special decentralized applications. *See* dApps and smart contracts as well as market capitalization

ethereum.org/en

fiat: any currency backed by a government as for example the United States dollar or the Swiss franc or the English pound. According to recent United Nations research there are 180 different government backed currencies. At the moment all of the cryptocurrencies are not backed by any government, but some are pegged to currencies considered safe such as the US dollar.

fork: a modification to the way a blockchain's software rules process, do valid transactions, or block. *See* hard and soft forks

gwei: just the way a US dollar has pennies, nickels, and quarters, gwei is the lowest coinage in the Ethereum currency.

hard fork: a modification to the rules that all nodes on a system must accept, or else depart from the network. *See* nodes

hash: a security process performed on data, files or messages to ensure that nothing has been corrupted, tampered or hacked. A good example is verifying that a signature on record is authentic and has not been changed.

HODL: abbr. hold on for dear life. A slang term used to advise an investor to hold on to the cryptocurrency investments even if the market price is falling.

hot wallet: in contrast to cold storage which has crypto assets stored offline, hot wallets are on the internet network so that tokens may be sent and received. If you want to buy for example an artwork, you need a hot wallet so that you can pay online for your purchase.

ICO: abbr. initial coin offering. A group or company seeking investors to buy tokens, sharing in the cost of creating a new coin, app, or service. There are at the moment no regulations or enforcement of securities laws for ICOs.

investment contract: the chairperson of the SEC, a branch of the United States government, recently announced that cryptocurrencies ". . . are part of an investment contract which meets the definition of a security under current law . . ." *See* SEC

ISP: abbr. internet service provider.

market capitalization in cryptocurrency: the value of the cryptocurrency figured by multiplying the price of the cryptocurrency with the number of coins in circulation.

mining: the action of persons who post cryptocurrency transactions and add them to the proof of work ledger. This process is validated on specialized computers known as nodes or mining rigs. Mining rigs are large banks of computers solely programmed to post the proof of work. Nodes refer to a singular computer or a bank of them which are not only able to post the proof of work transactions but also serve other functions. *See* proof of stake

mining rigs: high powered computers and banks of computers designed solely to mine for cryptocurrency.

NFT: abbr. non-fungible tokens. NFTs are not interchangeable. NFTs are objects such as diamonds, books, designer clothes, artwork or a video and thus have to be bought, sold or auctioned with currency.

nodes: *see* mining

private key: just as a password is used online to get into a bank account, a long complex password only known to the cryptocurrency owner is used to access his/her holdings.

proof of stake: staking is a way of earning yields from holding particular cryptocurrencies which have been invested via the blockchain. The proof of stake is the process of verifying these transactions without a bank or payment processor in the middle. This consensus mechanism allows users to hold their tokens while allowing them to authenticate transactions. If 51 percent or more don't agree, the block doesn't post.

public key: a wallet address online that can be shared with others thus enabling transactions similar to routing an account number for a bank account.

SAFT: abbr. simple agreement for future tokens. In the United States SAFTs are considered securities contracts. SAFTs must follow SEC regulations. The contract is an arrangement of when digital tokens are to be paid in the future to investors who provided capital to cryptocurrency developers. *See* SEC

satoshi: the smallest unit of a bitcoin much like a penny is the smallest unit in a dollar. There are approximately 100 million satoshis to a bitcoin. The satoshi is named after Satoshi Nakamoto, the founder of Bitcoin and blockchains. No one knows who Satoshi Nakamoto is. It may be a group of people or a single person. Whoever the group or the single person is, he/she/they want(s) anonymity and has or have so far succeeded in maintaining anonymity.

smart contract: may be installed and used on various blockchains. It carries out a series of commands on the blockchain. Smart contracts are not controlled by the user but rather by how they are programmed. It may be compared to a bank where you have set up a bill pay program which each month automatically pays your rent.

soft fork: a software upgrade that permits participants who did not upgrade to the new software to still use their original software in validating and verifying transactions.

stablecoin: a fixed priced cryptocurrency whose exchange worth is connected to another stable asset such as fiat currencies, or gold and other precious metals. *See* fiat

staking: much like locking up your money in a savings account or CD so that it can earn interest. Staking likewise is the act of placing crypto assets in an online account where it can earn interest in a designated cryptocurrency. *See* CD

tether: non-regulated cryptocurrency investments which according to the business behind it asserts that the outlay is secured by actual cash as US dollar, euros and/or other assets as gold, etc.

token: services or goods of value such as securities, real estate, etc., on a blockchain that have tradable assets.

USDC: abbr. United States dollar cryptocurrency. A tether which is backed one to one by liquid US dollar assets. *See* tether

USDT: abbr. US dollar/tether; backed by dollars. *See* tether

wallet: the user's data placed in a wallet reveals the user's cash location on the blockchain. The user can receive and spend money from his or her wallet via a cryptographic address issued by the wallet. Users may have more than one wallet based on the desired tokens.

wallet.dat: the file name commonly used on a hard drive to indicate backup information about an owner's public and private keys and other needed information. *See* public key and private key

web3: a world wide web site that caters to the blockchain principles, namely a decentralized internet with no central point of authority or control.

wei: a coin denomination in the Ethereum cryptocurrency. There are millions of wei(s) to one ether. *See* Ethereum

whale: individuals or establishments which hold sufficient large amounts of cryptocurrency to maneuver the market price.

XRP: a cryptocurrency positioned as an alternative to Bitcoin with faster and more energy-efficient transactions. Like all cryptocurrencies it is not backed by any government.

cointelegraph.com

ripple.com

FOR FURTHER READING

Before presenting a list of further reading for each chapter I would like to note that Google and Wikipedia are edifying sources. Most of the books used for resources in the original book, *Monarch's Dictionary of Investment Terms*, are still valid today. Throughout history most financial terms have remained classical. At the same time technology and the continual inventive aspects of business give unfailingly birth to new business words. These new words inspire and are popularized in new books and websites—many of which have been added to this **For Further Reading** section.

Bonds

Brindze, Ruth. *Investing Money: The Facts About Stocks and Bonds*. Harcourt, Brace and World, 1968.

Darst, David M. *The Complete Bond Book*. McGraw-Hill.

Davis, Lewis. *Dictionary of Banking and Finance*. Totowa, New Jersey: Rowman & Littlefield, 1978.

www.investopedia.com

www.wallstreetmojo.com
Understanding Bonds and Preferred Stocks. The New York Stock Exchange, Inc., 1978.

Stock Market Trading Terms

www.sec.gov/fast-answers
www.firsttrade.com/content/en-us/education/glossary
www.investopedia.com/articles/basics/03/103103.asp
www.nasdaq.com/articles/the-master-list-of-options-trading-terminology
www.bloomberg.com

Glossary of Stock Market Terms

www.nasdaq.com/glossary
www.sec.gov
www.theoptionsguide.com/stock-option.aspx
thebusinessprofessor.com
Barnes, Lee, Ph.D., and Feldman, Stephen, Ph.D., *Handbook of Wealth Management.* New York: McGraw-Hill Book Company, 1977.
Barnoff, Paul. *Wall Street Thesaurus.* Ivan Obolensky, 1963.
Eiteman, W. J., et al. Stock Market. 4th edition. McGraw-Hill, 1966.
Yasuyuki, Fuchita; Robert E. Litan (2006). *Financial Gatekeepers: Can They Protect Investors?.* Washington, D.C.: Brookings Institution Press.
Elliott, Ralph N. *An Elementary Introduction Into the Elliott's Wave Theory.* Institute of Economic Finance, 1981.

Flavian, C. *The College Student Introduction to the World of Wall Street*. American Classical College Press, 1974.

Goldberg, I, A. and Gordon, R. A. *How to Read Newspaper Stock Transactions*. Gordon, 1969.

Haft, Richard H. *Investing in Securities*. Englewood Cliffs, New Jersey: Prentice-Hall, Inc., 1975.

Hagin, Robert. *The Dow Jones-Irwin Guide to Modern Portfolio Theory*. Homewood, Illinois: Dow Jones-Irwin, 1979.

Language of Investing Glossary, The. The New York Stock Exchange, Inc., 1978.

Miller, Eugene. *Your Future in Securities*. Rosen Press, 1974.

Mitchell, Lloyd. *How to Make Money in Wall Street Through the Intelligent Use of Price Earning Ratios*. Institute of Economic Finance, 1981.

Standard & Poor's 500 Guide Annual

Stock Market & Wall Street: The Essential Knowledge Which Everybody But Absolutely Everybody Ought to Have Of the Stock Market and Wall Street. American Classical College Press (The Essential Knowledge Series Book), 1978.

Understanding Convertible Securities. The New York Stock Exchange, Inc., 1978.

Understanding the New York Stock Exchange. The New York Stock Exchange, Inc., 1976.

Weissman, Rudolph L. *The New Wall Street Facsimile*. Amo, 1975.

Commodities

imperiumcs.com/commodity-markets-glossary-terms

www.investopedia.com/terms/s/spreadoption.asp#toc-spread-option-examples

www.investopedia.com/terms/v/vanillaoption.asp

www.investopedia.com/terms/s/straddle.asp

Kroll, Stanley, and Shishko, Irwin. *The Commodity Futures Market Guide*. New York: Harper & Row, 1973.

Stevenson, Richard A. and Jennings, Edward H. *Fundamentals of Investments*. 2nd edition. St. Paul, Minnesota: West Publishing Co., 1981.

Teweles, Richard J., Ph.D.; Hurlow, Charles V., D.B.A.; and Stone, Herbert L., D.B.A. *The Commodity Futures Trading Guide*. New York: McGraw-Hill Book Co., 1969.

Wuliger, Betty S. *Dollar & Sense*. New York: Random House, 1976.

Money Instruments

Donoghue, William E., and Tilling, Thomas. *William E. Donoghue's Complete Money Market Guide*. New York: Harper & Row, 1980.

Greenwald, Douglas, and Associates. *The McGraw-Hill Dictionary of Modern Economics: A Handbook of Terms and Organizations*. New York: McGraw-Hill Book Co., 1973.

Stigum, Marcia. *The Money Market: Myth, Reality and Practice*. Homewood, Illinois 60430: Dow Jones-Irwin, 1978.

Diamonds, Gems, Valuable Coins, and Precious Metals

A Gold Pricing Model. International Gold Corporation Limited, 6455 Fifth Avenue, New York, N.Y. 10022

Beckner, Steven K. *The Hard Money Book*. New York: The Capitalist Reporter Press, 1979.

Carabini, Louis E., ed. *Everything You Need to Know Now About Gold and Silver*. New Rochelle, New York: Arlington House, 1974.

Gold Investment Handbook Statistical Update. International Gold Corporation Limited, 6455 Fifth Avenue, New York, N.Y. 10022

Green, Timothy. *How to Buy Gold*. New York: Walker & Co., 1975.

Matlins, Antoinette, P.G. & Bonanno, F.G.A., P.G., A.S.A. *Jewelry & Gems The Buying Guide 7th Edition*. Vermont: Gemstone Press (2009)

Persons, Robert H. *The Investor's Encyclopedia of Gold, Silver and Other Precious Metals*. New York: Random House, Inc., and MTS Publishing Corp., 1974.

Rogers, R. *Dictionary of Gems*. Birmingham: Jones & Palmer, Limited. 99+100 Albion Street, 1933.

Shipley, Robert Morrill. *Dictionary of Gems and Gemology*. Los Angeles, California: Gemological Institute of America, 541 South Alexandria, 1951.

Szuprowicz, Bohdan O. *How to Invest in Strategic Metals*. New York: St. Martin's Press, 175 Fifth Avenue, 1982.

Turner, W. W. *Gold Coins for Financial Survival*. Nashville, Tennessee: Hermitage Press, 1971.

Vilar, Pierre. *A History of Gold & Money*. London: NLB, 7 Carlisle St., W. 1, 1969.

Wise, Richard W. *Secrets Of The Gem Trade, The Connoisseur's Guide to Precious Gemstones*. Second Edition. Lenox, Massachusetts: Brunswick House Press, 2016

www.gia.edu/gem-encyclopedia

www.igi.org/gemblog

FOR FURTHER READING

Real Estate

Allen, Robert D., and Wolfe, Thomas E. *Real Estate Almanac.* New York: John Wiley & Sons, 1980.

Arnold Encyclopedia of Real Estate, The. Boston, Massachusetts: Warren, Gorham & Lamont, Inc., 1978.

Estes, Jack. *Real Estate License Preparation Course for The Uniform Examination.* New York: McGraw-Hill, Inc., 1976.

Gross, Jerome S. *Illustrated Encyclopedic Dictionary of Real Estate Terms.* Englewood Cliffs, New Jersey: Prentice-Hall, Inc., 1969.

Language of Real Estate, The. Chicago, Illinois: Real Estate Education Co., 1977.

Nessen, Robert L. *The Real Estate Book.* Boston: Little, Brown and Co., 1981.

Seldin, Maury, ed. *The Real Estate Handbook.* Homewood, Illinois: Dow Jones-Irwin, 1980.

Temple, Douglas M. *Making Money in Real Estate.* Chicago, Illinois: Henry Regnery Co.

Yoegel, John A. *Real Estate License Exams For Dummies* (4th edition). Hoboken, N.J.: John Wiley and Sons, Inc.

www.bankrate.com

www.law.cornell.edu/realestate

www.allbusiness.com

www.investopedia.com/real-estate-investing-guide

www.prepagent.com/real-estate-dictionary

Loans and Mortgages

Bryant, Willis R. *Mortgage Lending.* New York: McGraw-Hill Book Co., Inc., 1962.

160

Clontz, Ralph C., in collaboration with the editors of the Banking Law Journal. *Truth-In-Lending Manual*, revised edition. Boston, Massachusetts: Hanover Lamont Corporation, 1970.

Consumer Credit Guide. Chicago, Illinois: Commerce Clearing House, 1969.

Gross, Robin, and Cullen, Jean V. Help: *The Basics of Borrowing Money*. New York: Times Books, 1980.

Hayes, Rick Stephan. *Business Loans: A Guide to Money Sources and How to Approach Them Successfully*, 2nd ed. Boston, Massachusetts: CBI, d 1980.

How Much Do I Owe? How Much Can I Borrow?: A personal analysis and guide. New York: Dreyfus Publication, Ltd., 1972.

Reckley, Howard H. *Lending Functions of The Federal Reserve Banks: A History*. Washington Publications Services Division of Administrative Services. Board of Governors of the Federal Reserve System, 1973.

Income Opportunities. New York: Arco Publishing Company, 1964.

Jacoby, Neil Herman, and Saulnier, Raymond J. *Term Lending to Business*. New York: National Bureau of Research, 1942.

Johnson, Robert Willard; Johnson, Robert W.; Jordan, Robert L.; and Warren, William D. *Manual on the Federal Trust-In-Lending Law*. Washington, D.C.: National Foundation for Consumer Credit, 1969.

Mayer, Martin, and the editors of Dreyfus Publications. *Give Yourself Credit: The Art of Borrowing*; illustrated by Roy Doty. Dreyfus Publications, 1972.

Pease, Robert H., editor, and Kerwood, Lewis O., M.B.A., Associate editor. *Mortgage Banking*, 2nd edition. New York: McGraw-Hill Book Co., Inc. 1965.

Stevens, Mark. *Leveraged Finance: How to Raise and Invest Cash*. Englewood Cliffs, New Jersey: Prentice-Hall, 1980.

United States Commission on Federal Paperwork. Small Business Loans. For sale by the Superintendent of Documents, US Government Printing Office, 1977.

United States Small Business Administration. Investor Information Manual. Washington, D.C., 1980.

Insurance

Green, Thomas E. CPCU, CLU, ed.; Osler, Robert W.; Bickley, John S., Ph.D. *Glossary of Insurance Terms*. Santa Monica, California: The Merritt Company, 1661 Ninth Street, 1980.

Ingrisano, John R., ed. *The Insurance Dictionary, Life and Health Edition*. Indianapolis, Indiana: The Research and Review Service of America, Inc., 1978.

Kein, Marianne T. *Insurance Language*. Philadelphia, Pennsylvania: Running Press, 1949.

McIntyre, William Stokes, CP CU/ARM, ed. *Glossary of Insurance and Risk Management Terms*. Rimco, Inc., 1978.

www.investopedia.com/terms/i/insurance.asp

Financial Statements

Gibson, Charles H., and Boyer, Patricia A. *Financial Statement Analysis*. C.B.I. Publishing Co., Inc., Boston, Massachusetts 02210, 1979.

Hobbs, James B., D.B.A., and Moore, Carl L., M.A., C. P. A. *Financial Accounting*. South-Western Publishing Co., 1979.

Kendall, Jeffrey Slates. *Simplifying Accounting Language*. Dubuque, Iowa: Hunt Publishing Co., 1979.

Munn, Glenn G., revised and enlarged by F. L. Garcia. *Encyclopedia of Banking and Finance.* Boston: Bankers Publishing Co., 1973.

Understanding Financial Statements. Published by The New York Stock Exchange, Inc., with data compiled as of March 1981.

Investing In a Small Business

Albert, Kenneth J. *How to Pick the Right Small Business Opportunity.* New York: McGraw-Hill, 1977.

Allen, Louis L. *Starting and Succeeding in Your Own Small Business.* Foreword by Frank L. Tucker; Introduction by Wilford L. White. New York: Grosset & Dunlap, 1968.

Bennett, Vivo, and Clagett, Cricket. *1001 Ways to Be Your Own Boss.* Englewood Cliffs, New Jersey: Prentice-Hall, 1976.

Bentley Clark Associates, Office of Policy. Planning and Budgeting. Planning and Program Evaluation Division, US Small Business Administration, 1979.

Brannen, William H. *Successful Marketing For Your Small Business.* Englewood Cliffs, New Jersey: Prentice-Hall, 1978.

Bunn, Verne A. *Buying and Selling a Small Business.* Washington, D. C.: Small Business Administration, Superintendent of Documents, US Government Printing Office, 1969.

Bunzel, John E. *The American Small Businessman.* New York: Knopf, 1962.

Cahill, Jane. *Can a Small Store Succeed?* New York: Fairchild Publications, 1966.

Christensen, Carl Roland. *Management Succession in Small and Growing Enterprises.* Boston, Massachusetts: Division of Research, Graduate School of Business Administration, Harvard University, 1953.

Cole, Roland J., and Tegeler, Philip D. *Government Requirements of Small Business*. Lexington, Massachusetts: Lexington Books, 1980.

Dean, Sandra Linville. *How to Advertise: A Handbook for Small Business*. Wilmington, Delaware: Enterprise Publishers, 1980.

Dibble, Donald M., ed. *How to Plan and Finance a Growing Business*. Revised and updated edition. Fairfield, California: Entrepreveur Press, 1980.

Easley, Eddie V.; Lundgren, Earl F.; and Wolk, Harry I. *Contemporary Business: Challenges and Opportunities*. New York: West Publishing Co., 1978.

Fram, Eugene H. W. *What You Should Know About Small Business Marketing*. Dobbs Ferry, New York: Oceana Publishers, 1968.

Frantz, Forrest H. *Successful Small Business Management*. Englewood Cliffs, New Jersey: Prentice-Hall, 1978.

Gross, Eugene L.; Cancel, Adrian R.; and Figueroa, Oscar. *Small Business Works!* Illustrated by Eugene L. Gross. New York: Amacom, 1977.

Hammer, Marian Behan. *The Complete Handbook of How to Start and Run a Moneymaking Business in Your Home*. West Nyack, New York: Parker Publishing Co., 1975.

Key, Denise A., ed. *Encyclopedia of Associations*. Volume I, National Organizations of the US, 16th edition, Gale Research Co., Detroit, Michigan: Book Tower, 1981.

Lane, Marc J. *Legal Handbook for Small Business*. New York: Anacom, 1977.

Lowry, Albert L. *How to Become Financially Successful by Owning Your Own Business*. New York: Simon & Schuster, 1981.

Stanworth, M., and Curnan, V. *Management Motivation in the Smaller Business*. Epping: Gower Press, 1973.

Stevens, Mark. *36 Small Business Mistakes and How to Avoid Them*. West Nyack, New York: Parker, 1978.

Taylor, Frederick John. *How to Be Your Own Boss*. London: Business Books, 1975.

the-definition.com/business-studies

Cryptocurrency

Terrance, Lester. *The Cryptionary*. Lester Terrance, 2021.

financial-dictionary.thefreedictionary.com/business+dictionary

www.fcnb.ca/en/investing/high-risk-investments/crypto-assets-and-cryptocurrency

Token Economy, by Shermin Voshmgir, Kindle Edition, 2020.

www.theblockcrypto.com

cyberscrilla.com

www.fcnb.ca/en/investing/high-risk-investments/crypto-assets-and-cryptocurrency

www.nerdwallet.com/cryptocurrency

blockapps.net/blockchain-101-difference-ethereum-bitcoin

www.coindesk.com

hackernoon.com

www.nytimes.com/2022/03/08/us/politics/cryptocurrency-dao.html

hackernoon.com/what-is-apdao-c7e84aa1bd69

www.investopedia.com/terms/b/bitcoin-mining.asp

www.technologyreview.com/2018/04/23/143486/a-glossary-of-blockchain-jargon

cybersecurityglossary.com

www.wallstreetmojo.com

INDEX

INDEX

callable bond (*chapter* "Bonds")

callable stock (*chapter* "Stock Market Trading Terms")

cancellation (*chapter* "Insurance")

candlestick (*chapter* "Cryptocurrency")

capital (*chapter* "Financial Statements")

capital expenditure (*chapters* "Real Estate"; "Financial Statements")

capital gain (*chapter* "Real Estate")

capitalization method (*chapter* "Real Estate")

capitalization ratio (*chapter* "Financial Statements")

capitalize (*chapter* "Real Estate")

capital stock (*chapter* "Stock Market Trading Terms")

capital structure (*chapter* "Financial Statements")

carrier (*chapter* "Insurance")

carrying charges (*chapter* "Loans and Mortgages")

carryover clause (*chapter* "Real Estate")

cash disbursement journal (*chapter* "Financial Statements")

cash discount, *see* discount

cash flow (*chapter* "Financial Statements")

cash management fund, *see* CMA

cash receipts journal (*chapter* "Financial Statements")

cash refund annuity (*chapter* "Insurance")

cash sale (*chapter* "Stock Market Trading Terms")

cash surrender value (*chapter* "Insurance")

cash value (*chapter* "Insurance")

casualty insurance (*chapter* "Insurance")

catastrophe (*chapter* "Insurance")

caveat emptor (*chapter* "Real Estate")

CBDC central bank digital currency (*chapter* "Cryptocurrency")

CBOE (Chicago Board of Options Exchange) (*chapter* "Stock Market Trading Terms")

CD (certificate of deposit) (*chapters* "Money Instruments"; "Diamonds, Gems, Valuable Coins, and Precious Metals")

CDF (commercial deposit futures) (*chapter* "Commodities")

cede (*chapter* "Insurance")

centralized (*chapter* "Cryptocurrency")

certificate of insurance (*chapter* "Insurance")

certificate of deposit (*chapter* "Diamonds, Gems, Valuable Coins, and Precious Metals")

certificates (*chapter* "Stock Market Trading Terms")

Certified Public Accountant, *see* CPA

corporate bond equivalent (*chapter* "Bonds")

corporation (*chapter* "Investing in a Small Business")

correlation (*chapter* "Investing in a Small Business")

corridor deductible (*chapter* "Insurance")

cosigner (*chapter* "Loans and Mortgages")

cost effective rate, *see* advertisement cost of goods sold (*chapter* "Financial Statements")

costume jewelry (*chapter* "Diamonds, Gems, Valuable Coins, and Precious Metals")

counter-cyclical metal (*chapter* "Diamonds, Gems, Valuable Coins, and Precious Metals")

coupon (*chapter* "Bonds")

covenant (*chapter* "Real Estate")

coverage (*chapter* "Insurance")

covering (*chapter* "Stock Market Trading Terms")

CPA (Certified Public Accountant) (*chapter* "Financial Statements")

CPCU, *see* American Society of Chartered Property Casualty Underwriters

credit card (*chapter* "Loans and Mortgages")

credit information (*chapter* "Loans and Mortgages")

credit line (*chapter* "Loans and Mortgages")

credit investigator (*chapter* "Loans and Mortgages")

creditor (*chapter* "Loans and Mortgages")

credit risk (*chapter* "Bonds")

credit union (*chapter* "Money Instruments")

crypto (*chapter* "Cryptocurrency")

crypto assets (*chapter* "Cryptocurrency")

crypto coin (*chapter* "Cryptocurrency")

cryptocurrency (*chapter* "Cryptocurrency")

crypto discord server (*chapter* "Cryptocurrency")

cryptocurrency exchange (*chapter* "Cryptocurrency")

cryptography (*chapter* "Cryptocurrency")

CTP (*chapter* "Cryptocurrency")

CSO, *see* Commissioners Standard Ordinary

cumulative discount, *see* discount

cumulative preferred (*chapter* "Stock Market Trading Terms")

cumulative voting (*chapter* "Stock Market Trading Terms")

current assets (*chapter* "Financial Statements")

gem coin (coin grading) (*chapter* "Diamonds, Gems, Valuable Coins, and Precious Metals")

gem material (*chapter* "Diamonds, Gems, Valuable Coins, and Precious Metals")

gem mineral (*chapter* "Diamonds, Gems, Valuable Coins, and Precious Metals")

general public improvements (*chapter* "Real Estate")

general journal (*chapter* "Financial Statements")

general ledger (*chapter* "Financial Statements")

general mortgage, *see* blanket mortgage

general obligation bond (*chapter* "Bonds")

general partner(s) (*chapter* "Investing in a Small Business")

general public improvements (*chapter* "Real Estate")

genuine risk capital (*chapter* "Commodities")

germanium, *see* electronic metals

GIA Gemological Institute of America (*chapter* "Diamonds, Gems, Valuable Coins, and Precious Metals")

gilt-edged bond (*chapter* "Bonds")

Ginnie Mae (*chapter* "Bonds")

give up swap (*chapter* "Bonds")

GL (general liability) (*chapter* "Insurance")

going concern (*chapter* "Financial Statements")

gold (*chapter* "Diamonds, Gems, Valuable Coins, and Precious Metals")

gold and silver dealers (*chapter* "Diamonds, Gems, Valuable Coins, and Precious Metals")

gold bar (*chapter* "Diamonds, Gems, Valuable Coins, and Precious Metals")

gold bullion (*chapter* "Diamonds, Gems, Valuable Coins, and Precious Metals")

gold bullion coins (*chapter* "Diamonds, Gems, Valuable Coins, and Precious Metals")

gold coin (*chapter* "Diamonds, Gems, Valuable Coins, and Precious Metals")

gold standard (*chapter* "Diamonds, Gems, Valuable Coins, and Precious Metals")

good delivery (*chapter* "Stock Market Trading Terms")

good 'til canceled order (GTC or open door) (*chapter* "Stock Market Trading Terms")

goodwill, *see* intangible assets

governments (*chapter* "Bonds")

Government National Mortgage
 Association, *see* Ginnie Mae
grace period (*chapters* "Loans and
 Mortgages"; "Insurance")
graded commission (*chapter*
 "Insurance")
grading schedule for cities and towns
 (*chapter* "Insurance")
graduated life table (*chapter*
 "Insurance")
graduated mortgage payment (GPM),
 see mortgage (*chapter* "Loans and
 Mortgages")
graduated rental lease (*chapter* "Real
 Estate")
graph (*chapter* "Investing in a Small
 Business")
grossline (*chapter* "Insurance")
gross lease, *see* inclusive rent (*chapter*
 "Real Estate")
gross national product (GNP) (*chapter*
 "Investing in a Small Business")
gross premium (*chapter* "Insurance")
gross profit (*chapter* "Financial
 Statements")
gross sales (*chapter* "Financial
 Statements")
gross weight (*chapter* "Diamonds,
 Gems, Valuable Coins, and
 Precious Metals")
ground lease (*chapter* "Real Estate")
group insurance (*chapter* "Insurance")

growth stock (*chapter* "Stock
 Market Trading Terms")
GTC (good 'til canceled order or
 open door) (*chapter* "Stock
 Market Trading Terms")
guaranteed bond (*chapter* "Bonds")
guaranteed funds (*chapter*
 "Insurance")
guaranteed renewable (*chapter*
 "Insurance")
guarantor (*chapter* "Loans and
 Mortgages")
gwei (*chapter* "Cryptocurrency")

hangout (*chapter* "Loans and
 Mortgages")
hard fork (*chapter*
 "Cryptocurrency")
hard money mortgage, *see* mortgage
 (*chapter* "Loans and Mortgages")
hard products, *see* commodities
 (commodities)
hash (*chapter* "Cryptocurrency")
hazard (*chapter* "Insurance")
Health Insurance Association of
 America, *see* HIAA
Health Maintenance Organization,
 see HMO
heavy industry (*chapter* "Real
 Estate")
hectare (*chapter* "Real Estate")
hedge (*chapter* "Commodities")

ACKNOWLEDGMENTS

My thanks go to the many experts in the financial world who were willing to help me in my research. Among those who took time from their busy schedules to share their expertise were:

Cheryl Foote
realestateinsteamboat.com/about

Katheryn Pedersen
crosscountrymortgage.com/The-Pedersen-Team/Kathryn-Pedersen

Debbie Aragon
www.statefarm.com/agent/us/co/frisco/debbie-a-aragon-8ktrf8d1rgf

Neil Eigen
www.twst.com/bio/neil-t-eigen

Chris Slota, Lead Investment Analyst at Novel Capital, President at C4 Crypto Advisers
info@c4cryptoadvisers.com

Randy Rudasics, manager of the Yampa Valley Entrepreneurship Center (Colorado). Rudasics has assisted hundreds of entrepreneurs launch new businesses and is a former small business owner as well.

Perry Ninger has worn many hats in the financial world. His multitudinous positions include teaching finance and business at various western colleges and working as a CPA. He was employed for seventeen years by American Express in New York and Toronto. He was head of their global budgeting, and for a time managed their bond financing, their foreign exchange, and at one point oversaw their financial management.

Dorland Mountain Arts Colony deserves a big thank you for giving me space where I could spend long hours writing in peace and quiet. I especially appreciated their "we care" atmosphere.

I do want to say a few words about the first edition, the foundation for our present-day edition. So much has happened since this book came out in 1983. We have the use of personal computers and the internet. There are new types of investments which have given birth to a whole new string of investment terms such as ETFs and cryptocurrencies to cite a few. Some words mentioned in 1983 are obsolete and obviously have been taken out of this edition. However, I do not want to forget those who helped to vet the first edition. Richard Blodgett, Kenneth M. Fox, Donald Gross, Donald Fox, Peter C. Osborne, Jacques Luben, Sheridan Nofer, Neil T. Eigen, and E. B. Storms.

Very special thanks went to Professor Garland C. Owens, Ph.D., professor of accounting at the Graduate School of Business, Columbia University, a Certified Public Accountant, and business consultant. Professor Owens was the first one with whom I discussed the idea that a book explaining investment terms in simple language and in classified grouping was needed. He immediately encouraged the project and declared his readiness to help. Back then there was no internet and no books online. A writer's main resources were the libraries and experts in the field willing to talk to you.

The first edition included words of gratefulness to the Brooklyn Business Library as well as to the library of the American Institute of Certified Public Accountants. Merrill Lynch, Pierce Fenner and Smith, Inc., and Dean Witter Reynolds, New York Stock Exchange.

Some of the institutes who helped me zero into the important definition are no longer in existence, including the Chemical Bank, United States Trust Company of New York, Irving Trust, The New York Futures Exchange, and the American Stock Exchange.

ABOUT THE AUTHOR

Edith Lynn Hornik-Beer is an author and journalist. Her work has been published in such notable newspapers and magazines as the *Denver Post, New York Times, Elle,* and *Neue Zürcher Zeitung.* In 2017, she was among the winners of the Matt Kramer Award for Excellence in Journalism. Hornik-Beer is the author of several books, including *The Drinking Woman: Revisited* and *For Teenagers Living With a Parent Who Abuses Alcohol/Drugs.* She is now working on a historical novel.

www.essaysforthecuriousmind.com
www.thedrinkingwomanrevisited.com
www.answersforteens.com

OPEN ROAD

INTEGRATED MEDIA

Find a full list of our authors and
titles at www.openroadmedia.com

FOLLOW US
@OpenRoadMedia